JUST A MINUTE ...

A COLLECTION OF
SCOUTMASTER MINUTES

by Dave Tracewell

D1375327

Honor Publishing Company

P.O. Box 45643 • Kansas City • Missouri 64171 • USA

© 1995-99 by Dave Tracewell
All rights reserved under the Pan-American and
International Copyright Conventions

ISBN 0-967539-0-5-6

Published by
HONOR PUBLISHING COMPANY
P.O. BOX 45643
Kansas City, MO 64171

Printed in the United States of America

First Edition, First Printing

Book Layout by Pete Keppel
Cover Layout by Joni Schakel

Technical Assistance:
Kori Dillman
Jesse Candy

This book is dedicated to my Mother,
Alys Tracewell, who instilled in me,
long before I became a Scout,
the good that I have found in Scouting...

May her knowledge and wisdom
help me to help Scouts always.

CONTENTS

CHAPTER TWO: 12 MONTHLY RELIGIOUS MINUTES

CHAPTER THREE: TWELVE MONTHLY LEADER MINUTES

INTRODUCTION

As Scoutmaster of a Boy Scout Troop, and as an adult Scout leader for many years, I have been called upon to give brief stories or thoughts about pertinent subjects and problems that face our youth today.

Called the *Scoutmaster's Minute,* these short stories are used to spark a feeling about the subject you choose and provoke thoughts about how it will be used in the Scout's Troop, Patrol, family, or personal everyday life. Typically brief, these one to two minute stories, poems, or anecdotes will help to build the moral character of the youth in your Troop.

As an aid to your program, I have written 52 weekly Scoutmaster's minutes that you can use in your program, or, if you wish, use as reference to formulate your own versions.

This collection of short stories and parables that I have written, and a few that are from other sources, are about different situations that I have found to be useful as Scoutmaster's Minutes. They are designed for use as a short last message to be given to your Troop or youth group at the end of your Troop meeting, Patrol Leaders Council, or special occasion.

No Scouting activity should end without the Scoutmaster giving them a few moments of inspiration to tie into the activity that will help build character, promote citizenship, or offer challenges to his Scouts.

Some of these Scoutmaster's Minutes are fictional, and some are based on my experiences as Scoutmaster, and still some are just some poems, stories, or articles that I've come across during my term as Scoutmaster that I feel have been either inspirational or suitable to a situation. In any event, all are appropriate for use as inspirational or thought provoking "last" messages to Scouts and Scouters from your unit.

The Scoutmaster's Minute has been used by successful Scoutmasters for years as a final thought or comment to Troop meetings, Patrol Leader's Councils, Troop Campouts, Courts of Honor, and Scout's Own Services. It's use will leave a final impression on any event that will give your Scouts a fond or thought provoking memory.

I have separated the Scoutmaster's Minutes into three groups. The first group being 52 weekly "Minutes" used for events and meetings where the participants are primarily youth members, such as your regular Troop meetings, Campouts, Courts of Honor, etc.

The second group being 12 monthly "Minutes" appropriate for any Scout religious occasion such as a Scouts Own Service or special church services.

The third group being 12 monthly "Minutes" that are appropriate for use in adult training situations or committee meetings where adults are present.

Each message is "timed" to take between one and two minutes for delivery. The Scoutmasters Minute should be short, strong, yet inspirational. Messages much longer start to lose their importance and the Scouts attention.

Preempting the Scoutmasters Minute with certain "rules" can be effective once, and then only when necessary. "The Scoutmaster does not appreciate being timed" or "I want you to listen very carefully tonight, this is very important" are phrases that usually set the tone for deliverance.

Dave Tracewell

REMEMBER ME

I am here for you now.
Come be with me for you need me.

I'm here for just a little while.
Come talk to me for I have something to tell you.

I am here with you for only a short time.
Come walk with me for I have something to show you.

I am here just a little while longer.
Come stand with me for I need to make you ready to be without me.

I was here for only a short time.
Remember me.

David Tracewell

CHAPTER

1

52 WEEKLY SCOUTMASTER MINUTES

Week 1
The Aims of Scouting

The Boy Scout program works toward three aims:

One is growth in moral strength and character. We may define this as what a boy is to himself, his personal qualities, his values, his outlook on life.

A second aim is participating citizenship. Used broadly, citizenship means the boys relationship to others. He comes to learn of his obligations to other people, to the society he lives in, to the government that presides over that society.

A third aim of the Boy Scout program is development of physical, mental, and emotional fitness. Fitness includes the body: well tuned and healthy, the mind: able to think and solve problems, and the emotions: self control, courage, and self respect.

The methods are designed to accomplish these aims. Thus it is important that you know and use the methods of the Boy Scout program. Other methods are good but may bring different results, results quite different that we are seeking.

Take the time to learn what the Boy Scout program has to offer. Rely on the eighty-plus years of experience, the many hours of devotion by dedicated adults, and the training your fellow Scouts and Scout leaders have received to guide you and to become the best you can be.

Being a member of the worlds largest youth organization, joining in on the fun and adventure of Scouting, and achieving the aims and goals that the program offers are self rewarding and will help you to become a strong, well bred and respected man.

Week 2
A Scout Is ...

A Scout is adventurous, exciting, serious, fun, and a hundred other things too numerous to count. Scouting has taught honesty, loyalty, courage and service to others to millions of Scouts all over the world who have benefited from this phenomenal program.

You, as a Boy Scout and a member of the world brotherhood of Scouting, have a similar responsibility. You carry the expectation from people who know that you are a Scout, that you have a better understanding of the world around you, of being better prepared for emergencies, and of being more polite and courteous to the people you meet. Your position is one of responsibility and honor. This program is designed to help you meet and exceed those expectations.

Your participation in the Scouting program will help make you a better citizen, help you to learn and develop leadership skills, and help to keep yourself physically fit, mentally awake, and morally straight. By living the Scout Oath and Law, you will become an honest, unselfish citizen

People will come to admire and count on this trait. With your reverence toward God as your guide, the Scout program will help lead you down the right paths in life, and will give you a legacy that you and your family can be justly proud.

Week 3
Trustworthy

TRUST is a very interesting concept. Look at the Scout next to you... do you trust him? How about your Senior Patrol Leader, would you lend him a dollar? How about your Scoutmaster, is he trustworthy? Now ask yourself, what is the Scout next to me, my Senior Patrol Leader, or my Scoutmaster thinking about me? Am I a trustworthy person?

Billy Graham told a humorous story about trust and faith that I will share with you:

It seems a man was walking along a 100 foot cliff and suddenly stumbled and fell off the cliff. In desperation, he grabbed the only thing he could, a branch of a small bush growing in the side of the cliff. Well, his cries of help could not be heard, and he was losing his grip when suddenly, he heard a loud booming voice from above:

"THIS IS THE LORD, MY SON. DO YOU BELIEVE IN ME?"

"Oh yes," said the man, "yes, please help me. I can't hold on much longer. Thank God you've heard me. Hurry!"

"WELL, IF YOU BELIEVE IN ME, AND YOUR FAITH IS STRONG, TRUST ME AND DO AS I SAY"

The man again said "yes... yes, I believe in you, please help me as I can't hold on any longer!

To this the Lord said:

"LET GO OF THE BRANCH, AND I WILL SAVE YOU."

The man looked down at the ground 100 feet below, looked at the branch he was hanging onto, and then looked slowly towards the heavens and said:

"Is there anyone else up there I could talk to?"

Earning someone's trust is not easy, but if you just do what you say you will do, and live by the Scout Law you can be known as a trustful person. But if you ever lose someone's trust in you, you may never be able to fully regain it. Are you a trustful person? What can you do to make people trust you even more?

Week 4
Loyal

As Scoutmaster, I've often asked my Scouts what loyalty means. I get some pretty interesting answers. Are you loyal to your country? To your school? To your family? The answer is usually "yes," but what does it really mean?

When I was a Scout, (yes they did have Scouts when I was a teenager), I was Patrol Leader, and had 5 Scouts in my Patrol. Two of the Scouts in my patrol, the Hawk Patrol, went to another School, a rival of the school that I attended. Well, when it came to football season, there was a difference of opinion as to who's football team was the best. A few of us, including myself, were on the opposing football teams at school, and we were always saying "our" team was the best.

When it came time to play each other in the "big" game, it seemed that each of us played a little harder that day to prove "we were the best." Well, we were the best... best friends that is. I don't even remember who won, but I do remember Dennis and Randy, and the rest of the Scouts in "my" patrol. Even though they were loyal to their school teams, when they were in our patrol, they were loyal to the Hawk Patrol, and loyal to me as my friend.

Loyalty is the strength in one's friendship, the strength in your commitment to what ever you are doing. Many men thoughout history have shown their loyalty to their country by giving up their lives in the protection of their country, their family, and in their beliefs.

- *Be loyal to your family, Troop, Community, and Country by helping and supporting it's members, say you are proud to be associated with them.*

- *Be loyal by obeying the laws of your community and helping it's citizens, and by continuing to learn more about your country and it's great heritage.*

- *Be proud of being an American, and a member of the largest youth organization in the world, The Boy Scouts of America.*

Week 5
Helpful

Remember how Scouting got started in the United States? It was by one Scout being helpful to a lost businessman in the dense London fog to reach his destination. That one helpful act brought Scouting to millions of boys in our country.

In every country the aim "being helpful" means more than just helping out around your house, or doing things for your Troop. It means doing things for other people willingly, at all times, without asking for money or a reward.

Baden-Powell has stated:

"In every country the aim of a Scout's training is identical, namely, efficiency for service toward others; and with such an object in common, we can, as an international brotherhood of service, go forward and do a far reaching work."

Remember your Scout promise to "help other people at all times" and your Scout slogan "To do a good turn daily." These are not just "words" for you to remember, but are a things you should do in your everyday life.

The Scouting program is designed to help you become better prepared to help people in times of need. Learning first aid and CPR, how to live and survive in the outdoors, and how to read a map and get around your community are just some of the skills you have or will learn that will make you better prepared to be helpful to the people around you.

As a Scout, people will expect you to be helpful, and will feel confident that you will be able to "handle" the task. To be truly helpful it will be up to you to learn as many worthwhile skills as you can.

But remember, it's OK to work for money, but it is not considered a "Good Turn" if you get paid. Helping people and doing good turns will bring you many rewards that can never be measured in dollars and cents. Nothing makes a person feel better than when he has the ability to help someone and has done so successfully.

Week 6
Friendly

A Scout is friendly. That's one of the laws you say every time you repeat the Scout Law. But how friendly are you? When was the last time you were friendly to someone or made a new friend? You should seek out people who are most like the person you would like to be, good people who have the same ideals and values you deem important, and become their friend. You should strive always to be friendly towards everyone you meet.

The one thing you can always give to someone, that won't cost you a dime, and will usually be returned immediately is what?

Yes, a smile!

Greeting people with a friendly smile, and sincere intentions, will usually gain you many people who would like to be your friend. Take the time to get to know these people, and pick the ones that you feel will be the "best" for you. Then take the time to grow into a great friendship with these people and they will be your friends for a long time.

Being friendly also means "just doing nice things" for everyone, not just your friends. Helping around the house, helping someone who has dropped something, carrying in the groceries for your neighbor, or just simply being nice to someone are good examples of being friendly.

Think about how you have been friendly today... yesterday... and how you can be even friendlier tomorrow. You will be amazed at how many friends you get as a reward for being friendly.

Week 7
Courteous

Courtesy is a true sign of character. How you treat the people around you says a lot about you. To be polite and courteous to others shows that you care about others and what they think about you. Doing things like saying please and thank you, opening the door for women, and not using foul or abusive language marks you as a true gentleman, something every young man can be proud of.

I remember traveling on a bus this last summer in Yosemite National Park with our Scout Troop, and at every stop, people would get off and then a group would get back on. At one of these stops, more people got on than off, leaving all of the seats taken, and people standing in the aisles. It was a true sense of pride for me to see four Scouts get up simultaneously and offer their seats to some elderly people who had just boarded the bus. As we got off the bus, one of them turned to me and said "Those are some fine young men you have there, keep up the good work."

When people know you are a Scout, or see you wearing the Scout Uniform, they come to expect courtesy and politeness from you. It is up to you to live up to their expectations and make your family and friends proud of you. Nothing shows the character and upbringing of a child more than how they treat the people around them. Be polite and courteous to everyone you meet and know. Be proud to be known as a gentleman. Live up to the expectations that come with wearing a Scout uniform.

Week 8
Kind

Kindness comes in many forms. A kind act may be helping a person in need, it could be pulling a thorn out of an animals paw, or possibly, just talking to an elderly person who is lonely. If you are kind and loving towards animals, and show a high regard for life, then you are living up to your promise to obey the Scout Law. It is wrong to purposely hurt or harm any living thing.

I once had a Scout who used to love to tease and torture small animals and insects. I won't go into details, but needless to say, he did not treat them kindly, and this reflected also in the way he treated his parents, family, and friends. As he grew older, he eventually quit Scouting, and wound up in juvenile hall for assault and battery on one of his schoolmates. He let the meanness in him take control of his judgment and his life.

Being known as a kind person, one who is known to help and comfort those in need, is certainly an admirable quality. By being known as a kind person, people will come to trust and respect you. You won't have to worry about telling people about your kind deeds, in fact, to do so would probably cause more doubt than admiration. Just lead your life in a kind manner and good things will come to you. Being gentle and kind is one quality that will always come back to you magnified by your deeds.

Think about some ways you can be a kinder and more gentle person, how you can help to make a difference in making your house, your community, and your country a nicer place to live.

Week 9
Obedient

Some of us are obedient out of fear: fear of punishment from our parents, employers, or, perhaps, even our God. Some of us obey out of respect. Respect for someone's authority, knowledge, or position, whatever your motivation, obedience is important in our lives.

You should always respect your parents by obeying their rules and wishes. You must first evaluate what is being asked of you, then discuss anything that you feel is of importance, then do what you are told. Build a trusting relationship with your parents. Only ask questions about what you are told when you think there may be a better way or some concern in their request.

Otherwise, do what you are told or expected to do, when you are supposed to do it. It is the only course of action. Not to do so will cause even more distrust and problems. If it happens to be your employer, you could even lose your job.

Remember, you are responsible for your own actions, and obedience is the best way to build trust and confidence in the eyes of those who you respect.

Go home tonight and tell those in your family that you love them, and show it by obeying the rules of your house and doing what is expected of you, and a little bit more.

Week 10
Cheerful

Have you ever met a person who is always happy? Someone you love to be around? We all have... it's fun to be around them, and any work or tasks that need to be done seem a lot easier when we do them with this person. Cheerfulness is contagious. We get it, or spread it to those around us.

If you have a cheerful manner, and spread that to the people around you, people will want to be with you. You will feel better about yourself, and will be healthier. Think about it, people are seldom sick when they are happy.

Abraham Lincoln, our 16th President and one of our countries greatest leaders once said:

"I smile and I smile, as one by one the crowd passes by to shake my hand. It seems it's a week before I get my face all straightened out again, but it is my duty. I could defeat the whole army tomorrow by looking glum at a reception or refusing to smile for three hours at a time."

He knew how important it was for a leader to keep a cheery disposition, even when things weren't going exactly right. The good leader spreads his cheerful manner until all those around him want to help and soon, the problem is solved.

Go home tonight and look into the mirror. Do you see a happy person? Think about what you can do to make your life happier, and how you can make your family members and friends happier. Try greeting everyone you meet with a warm smile. You'll be surprised at how many you get in return.

Week 11
Thrifty

It's really quite simple. Being thrifty means spending less, not more than you make or earn, learning not to waste what you have, and use all that you take.

The Indians of central California were some of the best conservationists in the world, long before it became "fashionable" to be so. They learned to replace that which they took from the earth so that they would never want.

When they killed a deer for food, literally every part of the animal was used. The meat for food, the hide for clothing and shoes, the sinew for bow strings, the blood for paint and medicine, the hoofs for baby rattles. Even the brains were mixed with local plants to tan the leather hides. The bones were used for tools, needles, and combs.

Everything was used, not thrown away. They had no need or use for garbage dumps, everything they ate, drank, or used was biodegradable.

As a Scout, you should strive to set an example of being thrifty by only buying items which you need. Think ahead about your wants and needs. Plan your purchases so that your money isn't wasted on items that are cheap and will not give you good service. Spend wisely the money you earn, and save your money when you can.

Go home tonight and look around at all of the things you've obtained during the last year that you do not use any longer. How many things did you buy that broke soon after purchasing them? If you would have waited and bought a little better quality item, would you still have and be using it today? Look in your garbage can and see how much waste there is.

Can you do anything to help keep this waste to a minimum... can you recycle your aluminum cans, glass, and newspapers? Think of the Indians... and then think of what you can do to make a difference in your home.

Week 12
Brave

As reported in Boys Life many years ago, a young 14 year old Scout by the name of Allen Daggett from Oakland, California gave his life to save his younger brother from being killed by a train. Just before he died, after he found out his little brother was all right, he regained consciousness just long enough to say "I couldn't have done anything else... I'm a Scout" with the word "Scout" being the last word he ever said.

He lived by his "actions" as a Scout, not just his word. There have been many heroes though out history who have given up everything, including their lives, for their Country, family, and friends. I'm not saying you need to get killed to prove how brave you are, but I am saying that you need to prepare yourself physically and mentally so that you will be able to help if and when the time comes that your Scouting skills are called upon to help someone in need. Your training now will be your guide then, when you need it the most.

Now think for a moment... think of what you would do if you came upon a horrible accident on your way home tonight. Do you think you would be the one who would be able to help, or would you be one of the people watching? If someone was in a life threatening situation, would you have the courage and know how to be able to get them out in the safest manner, or would you just have to stand there and let them die?

Only you can answer these questions. Each one of you is different. But think about what you, as a Scout, must do to make yourself better prepared to deal with these types of emergencies, and then take steps to get the training needed to make yourself a better Scout and a more courageous person.

From "A Scouter's Minute"
published by the LDS Church

Week 13
Clean

A Scout is Clean... what does that really mean? Yes, we all know it means that we need to take a bath or shower every day, and that we need to wear clean clothes. We need to wash our hands before we handle or eat food, that's only common sense. Being a clean person in "that" sense will keep us healthier and keep us from offending people around us. But, there are other ways of being clean that we must consider.

When was the last time you used a "bad" word? Do you hang out with friends whose every other word is a "four letter" word? Do you use profanity on a regular basis? This type of "clean" is also very much part of the Scout Law that you must live by.

It takes a lot "tougher" Scout to tell your friends that you don't like that type of language and don't want to hear it than the Scout who is trying to show how "tough" he is by using it. Keep your language clean as well as your body.

Now, what about your room at home? Is it clean? Do you do your part at home to keep it clean and presentable for your parents? Do you do your chores with out having to be told to, or do your parents have to keep telling you to clean your room, mow the lawn, or whatever? Another part of being clean is keeping your room and home clean as well.

And finally, do you have a "clean mind?" Are you involved with drugs, stealing, cheating, or pornography? If not, good! That's what I would hope and expect, but if you are, you need to get help and start living up to that part of the Scout Law of being clean right now!

Be Clean... not only in mind and body, but in everything you do that effects the world around you.

Week 14
Reverent

Look at a U.S. coin, or a dollar bill. Somewhere on them are the words "In God We Trust." Our country's forefathers thought that it was so important to include a reference to God in our country that they included it on every coin, and on every denomination of money we have, something that everyone handles every day.

The values, which the Boy Scouts of America strives to instill in young people, are those based upon the Scout Oath and the Scout Law. A Scout pledges:

"On my honor I will do my best, to do my duty to God and my country, and to obey the Scout Law ..."

The first "Boy Scouts of America Handbook for Boys," published in August 1911, declares that ..". no boy can grow into the best kind of citizenship without recognizing his obligation to God."

The tenth edition of "The Official Boy Scout Handbook," published in 1989 (page 561) reads: "A Scout is reverent toward God. He is faithful in his religious duties. He respects the beliefs of others."

While not intending to define what constitutes belief in God, the Boy Scouts of America is proud to reaffirm the Scout Oath and its declaration of "Duty to God."

The Boy Scouts of America has always been committed to the moral, ethical, and spiritual development of our youth. Scouting is not a religion, but duty to God is a basic tenet of the Scout Oath and Law. Scouting does not seek to impose its beliefs upon others who do not share them. Virtually every religion is represented in Scouting and the BSA does not define or interpret God. That is the role of the Scout's family and religious advisors.

Scouting respects those who do not share its beliefs and it would not ask others to alter their faith in any fashion in order to become Scouts. They too are free to follow their own beliefs. Rather, the BSA membership believes that the principles set forth in the Scout Oath and Law are central to the BSA goal of teaching the values of self reliance, courage, integrity, and consideration to others.

Week 15
Duty to God

"On my honor I will do my best, to do my duty, to God..."

So goes the first part of the Boy Scout Oath and promise, a promise you have probably made at least a hundred times. Have you ever wondered what it is you are promising, and promising it to God?

Well, lets think about it for a minute... what "duty" do you owe to God? Winston Churchill, the great Prime Minister of Great Britain, said:

"The fulfillment of spiritual duty in our daily life is vital to our survival."

This means simply giving thanks to God at mealtimes for the food and drink you have, saying thanks for your health, home, and family, and perhaps just saying thank you to God for something nice that happens to you.

Your duty to God also means living up to your commitments and doing good to and for others. Do things as if God is standing behind you, and live by your religious convictions and laws.

Remember, your Scout Oath is a promise, a promise which contains a "promise" to God that you will do your best. This is a promise that shouldn't be taken lightly.

Week 16
Duty to your Country

Your country has a long and noble history of men and women who have served their country and protected it's values. Many men have fought and died for their country and your freedom. A freedom that most people in this country now take for granted. Let's talk about freedom and what it means to you.

Have any of you gone on vacation out of state? Was there any problem going from one state to another? Probably not. Can your parents buy any car they choose, or go shopping on any day they like? These are all "freedoms" that some countries don't allow their citizens, "freedoms" that we have fought long and hard for and must protect.

Your Duty to your country means that you are willing to help fight for this freedom, to help keep it clean, and to strengthen it by becoming a good citizen.

Every one of you can make a difference. Everyone of you must realize that the freedom we have was paid for by the thousands of men and women who gave up their lives fighting for that freedom.

There may come a day when your country will ask you, too, to come to the aid of our country in defending that freedom. It will be your duty to be prepared and step forward if and when that time comes. By learning all you can in the Scouting program now, you will be better prepared to meet that challenge, should it ever come.

Week 17
Duty to Yourself

It's great to be helpful, and do things for other people, but you have to remember, that first, you have to take care of yourself. When you take care of yourself, build and keep your body in it's best shape, learn all that you can, and strive to be successful, then you will be better prepared to offer help and guidance when it's needed.

Your assistance will be considered more valuable if you have the strength, knowledge and ability to not only perform the tasks given, but to take charge and lead others to be helpful as well.

If you haven't spent the time to properly prepare yourself, then you may not achieve the degree of helpfulness you would like, and may actually make matters worse.

It's your responsibility to make yourself the "best that you can be" first! You have learned, or will learn a great deal on your Scouting trail. Be serious, take the time to learn what is being offered.

Take pride in knowing that the help and service that you have to offer your school, your home, your Troop, and eventually, your country is the best help available and that you have done everything you could do to make yourself, "Physically Strong, Mentally Awake and Morally Straight."

Week 18
Friends

Robert Baden-Powell once said: "The way to have friends is first to be one"* and to be a friend is a responsibility not to be taken lightly. To be a friend means being someone who others can be rely on, one that people can trust, and will "be there" when needed.

Look around you, think about the people you know at school, and in your neighborhood, and count the real friends that you have. It's quite possible that many of your "best" friends are right here in your Troop. The wealthiest among us are those who have many friends.

Remember that a Scout is a friend to all. He must offer his friendship to all Scouts and give them the sense that he really cares about them. By feeding and nurturing your friendships, they will grow into lifelong friends that will be with you always.

Making friends is not really that hard. It just takes a little effort on your part to introduce yourself, and get to know someone. You can start by getting to know the Scouts in your own patrol. Find out what their strengths and weaknesses are. If they need help in an area you know well, then help them. In the same way, if you need help in an area, there may be someone in your patrol who would be willing to help you. That's what friendship is all about. You not only make your patrol stronger by helping each other, but you can also gain more friends by meeting their "other" friends as well.

Making friends is easy, keeping friends takes a little work. You must act quickly and fairly to resolve any differences or problems that arise. The lack of communication, respect and tolerance are usually the biggest problems that break up friendships.

Being a friend means "keeping in touch," respecting other peoples wishes and privacy, and tolerating their little faults. Being there in a supporting and helpful way when needed, and letting your friends know that you care is the best way to keep friends.

One word of caution though, be careful of the friends you make, as there are some who will claim to be a friend only to desert you in time of need. One that will claim friendship, only to be quick to put the blame on you rather than "stick up" for you. "Fair Weather" friends who are only friends when it suits them should be avoided.

It takes time to make a "good" friend, so take time to pick the best people you want as your friends. Pick people who hold the same values that you think are important, then develop your friendship with them.

Now, again, take a look around you, think of the people you know at school and in your neighborhood, and count your friends. Now think of who you would like to be friends with and make an effort to go out and make new friends this week. Only YOU can do it, the friends you make today can last a lifetime... Good Luck!

*Quoted in the Handbook for Boys, 1946 edition, page 9

Week 19
Teamwork

Everyone put up their hand and stretch your fingers wide in front of you. Are each of your fingers important? Would you be as strong if you lost any of them? Now make a clenched fist. It is even stronger isn't it. If you don't believe it, think of how a boxer would do if he used his fingers to fight with instead of his fists. Now, think of your hand, and your fingers as your patrol. If your missing any of them, you are not as strong! But, if you all work together, you become stronger!

I challenge all of you to pull together and form a strong team out of the Scouts in your patrol.

Once everyone in your patrol gets to know one another, and trust one another, then you can start becoming friends that help each other. Some will be great at knots, others pretty good at map and compass, and still others who love to cook. As a team, you make a great patrol. You begin to not only trust one another, but count on each other to help out in certain situations.

As a team, working together, using each others strengths to your advantage, you make YOUR Patrol the best it can be. Like the clenched fist, you become stronger and better at what you are doing. The team can't be strong if some are missing, so urge everyone in your patrol to make all events and meetings.

If a member isn't there, you, and your patrol lose an important part of your team. If you don't get to know all the Scouts in your Patrol, and what their strengths are, then your team will never be able to make the best use of each others strong points.

Get to know the Scouts in your patrol, and let them do what they do best. And finally, become friends and help each other in any way you can to make your patrol the Best!

Sketch by Baden-Powell

Week 20
Honesty

Some of you are not very honest sometimes. Some are honest part of the time, and others are honest most of the time. But, probably, there is not one of you who has not told a lie, stolen something, or has cheated on a test at least once in their life. It may, or may not have happened to you. The important point I'm making is that we must all strive to become honest, and be known to all as an honest person.

Think back at the last time you told a lie. Not very proud of it are you? And telling one lie often leads into telling other lies to cover up the first one, and so we start to get trapped in our own lies. Some of you may have even stolen something, a piece of candy at the store, maybe some change off your parents dresser at home. Some of you may have cheated on a test at school, or maybe cheated a friend out of some money. These are things that mark you, if you get caught, for the rest of your life as a person who can't be trusted or is dishonest. Is it worth it? NO!

But you can do something about it. RIGHT NOW!, Yes, starting right now, start thinking of yourself as a honest person, and start telling the truth, no matter how hard it is. People will respect you for telling the truth, a lot more than if they catch you in a lie. Cervantes said it in the sixteenth century, and it still holds true today, "Honesty is the best Policy."

Go home tonight, and look in the mirror... and ask yourself if you are the person you want to be.

Ask yourself if you are an honest person, and if answer is no, then tell yourself that starting now you will become that person you want to be, an honest person that you are proud to look at in the mirror.

Week 21
Parents

Your Mom and Dad are special. Some of you may only have one of them living with you right now, some of you may have someone taking the place of your parents right now, and if that's true, they are pretty special too.

I know your parents care for you. That's one of the reasons you are here in this Troop and in the Boy Scout program. They want the best for you, and are proud of you each time you advance in rank or bring home another Merit Badge or award.

That, in itself, gives you all the more reason to do good in the Scouts and to push yourself harder to advance. But just doing the best you can, looking the best you can, and having fun doing it will also make your parents proud of you. This goes for anything you do, whether it's in Scouting, school, Church, or other activities.

Your parents give you their name, a place to stay, they feed you, teach you how to avoid the mistakes they made and punish you when you get in trouble. However, they love you enough to help you out of it, praise you when you do good, and give you presents on your birthday and during Christmas time. They are pretty special people.

If you can say to yourself that "I am a credit to my parents and my name, that I do things that they are proud of, and that I honor my Mom and Dad by being and doing my best," then you can say that you "LOVE" them, and they can truly be proud to call you their son.

Week 22
Home

"Be it ever so humble, there's no place like home." The immortal words of John Howard Payne strike a true note every time I hear them. Think about it... where is the most important place in your life? Where do you always return? A place where you can go anytime you want... to eat, sleep, watch TV, or maybe just find some peace and quiet. There's love there... your own private world. Your father's castle, your mothers world, the safest place on earth for you. You celebrate birthdays, anniversaries, Thanksgiving, and Christmas there.

Now lets think about your home. What is your "role" there? Your father and mother probably work to earn money so you can live there. Maybe just one or the other, but they do have to work hard to be able to give you a place to stay. Maybe your mother takes the time to cook your dinner every night... maybe she spends her day cleaning up and taking care of your house.

What do you do? What can you do? Do you have chores? Do you have to be told to do them?

Remember. it's your home, and like taking care of yourself, dressing nicely, or simply just taking a bath, your house needs to be taken care of as well. It's not expensive furniture, it's not a big house, nor living in the best part of town that makes a great home. It's the love you find at home from your mom, dad, your brothers and sisters, and respect that you give your family and the place you live.

And so my young friends, I leave you tonight with a little poem that came out of the New York Times a long time ago:

So long as there are homes
to which men turn at the close of day;
So long as there are homes
where the children are, where women stay;

If love and loyalty and faith
be found across those sills,
A stricken nation can recover
from its gravest ills.

So long as there are homes
where fires burn and there is bread,
So long as there are homes
where lamps are lit and prayers are said;

Although a people falter
through the dark, and nations grope,
With God Himself back of these little homes,
we have sure hope.

Week 23
Fun

One of the reasons you joined Scouting was to "HAVE FUN." But fun comes in many forms. What is "fun" to someone else, may be stupid to you, or against the law. Other types of "fun" will help build you physically and mentally. One of the things you have or will learn in Scouts is that there are many ways that you can have good clean fun.

Games and competitions will not only be a lot of fun to do, but will be educational and physically challenging as well. Or maybe your idea of fun is going camping, hiking, rock climbing, or swimming. Maybe it's just earning rank advancements or merit badges. Or some of you might think it's a lot of fun to take a fifty mile hike in the wilderness. More than likely, most of you will think all or most of these things are fun, and that's why you are staying in Scouting.

Now, if you aren't doing all of these things, and you want to, then you have discovered one of the best kept secrets in Scouting... YOU need to plan your program to have fun! Yes, I said you! The Scouts plan the program, and we, as adults, advise and support YOUR program.

Sometimes it takes a lot of planning to make sure you have a lot of fun, and that's what your Patrol Leaders and Senior Patrol Leader should be doing at your Patrol Leaders Council – planning your fun. Think back at some of the best times you've had in Scouting... was it a planned event, maybe a summer camp or camporee, or was it a program or event that "just happened"?

Sometimes they do *just happen,* and that's great! But most likely, the best times you've had were planned events with lots of games and competition, or a campout or hike that was planned well in advance. If you plan the programs ahead of time, you can almost guarantee a great time on every event.

So tonight, before you leave, ask your Patrol Leader, or Senior Patrol Leader what "fun" they have planned for you in the near future. If they can't answer that question... then maybe you can give them some suggestions by your next meeting. Have Fun!

Remember...Baden-Powell said
"If it isn't Fun, it isn't Scouting..". if your not having fun... your not doing it right!

Week 24
Participation

Participation by everyone in a program is vital to it's survival. Some of you are on sport teams at school. What do you think would happen if your quarterback didn't show up at a football game? What if the pitcher in a baseball game didn't play? The teams wouldn't do so well. It's the same thing with your patrol. If some of your patrol members don't show up to the meetings, it's you that suffers, and your patrol isn't as strong.

Put your hand up in front of you and spread your fingers. Move them around, make a fist, they work pretty well together don't they? You could say they make a good team. Now imagine that you were missing some of them... your hand wouldn't work as well would it? That's what happens when some of the Scouts in your patrol don't show up.

It's up to every member of the patrol, not just the patrol leader, to call and remind the friends in their patrols to show up. How can you make proper plans for events when you don't know how many to plan for?

Participation by everyone in your patrol will make your patrol stronger, your Scouting experience better, and your events a lot more fun.

Week 25
Killing

Once, when I was about 14 years old, I went hunting with my father for the first time. He had bought me a brand new 22 cal. rifle for the occasion, and I had practiced until I was quite good at shooting bottles and cans. I would line them all up on a rock or a fence about 100 feet away, and then fire at them until I could hit any one of them on my first shot. It felt good when my dad would brag at how good I had become. And then came the day when we would go hunting.

During the first day in camp I happened to see a bushy tailed blue squirrel climbing a tree about 150 feet away. I grabbed my rifle, took careful aim, and fired! Blam!, got him right in the back of the head, a good clean shot. The squirrel dropped to the ground dead, and I ran excitedly over to the small animal, praising myself for being such a good shot until I reached him. And there, on the ground, in front of me, lay a lifeless little squirrel that was just a few moments before frolicking from limb to limb on the tree above. I had killed him, for no reason other than to see how good a shot I was.

I have always regretted that useless killing, and although I have spent many other hunting trips with my dad, have yet to hunt and kill any other living thing since that time.

Killing for a purpose, ie: for food, clothing, or protection is one thing, and is a part of life. But to kill for no apparent reason is irresponsible and cruel.

In our society today we see a lot of killing and violence in the movies, and in the television programs we watch. We must keep in perspective the fact that these scenes are for our entertainment, and not for emulation.

You must remember that to kill is wrong, and that it is YOU that has to make up your mind what is good and what is bad.

You will always be held accountable for your own actions. Think of how useless the killing of that squirrel was, how a once happy little squirrel was shot for no good reason, and how you would feel if it was you that pulled the trigger.

Week 26
Pride

Most of you have brothers or sisters at home, and some of you get along with them better than others, but if someone outside your family called them names or did something to hurt or embarrass them, you would more than likely be upset about it. What if someone said something bad about your mother or father, or your family name? You would probably say or do something about it. That's because you take "pride" in your family name. Each of us has a certain amount of dignity and self respect that we feel we must protect if it becomes necessary.

Now what about the Scouts in your patrol? Is your patrol the best patrol? Are your willing to "stick up" for them, or are you one of the Scouts teasing and putting them down? Are you proud to be a member of your patrol or are you always saying bad things about it to your friends?

What about your troop? Is your troop the "best" troop? Are you proud to be a part of it? Take "pride" in making yourself, and the Scouts in your patrol, the best Scouts you can be, your patrol the best patrol, and your troop the best troop in your Council.

Don't pick on the young or smaller Scouts in your patrol, be their friend, and let them know that you will help and stick up for them if it's necessary. Become a "big brother" to them, and see to it that they advance in Scouting and have fun.

In whatever you do, take pride in making it the best! Be proud of what you accomplish, and help the people around you to be "their best." Always be proud to be associated with the Scouts in your patrol and troop, and take pride in announcing or discussing their progress or accomplishments.

In whatever you do, take pride in making it the best.

Week 27
Patriotism

"The American's Creed"

*"I believe in the United States of America as a government of the people,
by the people, for the people; whose just powers are derived from the consent
of the governed; a democracy in a republic and a sovereign nation of many
sovereign states; a perfect union, one and inseparable; established upon those
principles of freedom, equality, justice, and humanity for which American
patriots sacrificed their lives and fortunes.
I, therefore, believe it is my duty to my country to love it, to support its constitution,
to obey its laws, to respect its flag and to defend it against all enemies."*

These words are as true now as when they were written by William Tyler Page in 1917*. Patriotism for ones country is what makes us fight for what it stands for. Its what makes us feel that "rush" of pride when we hear our National Anthem, what makes us proud to be an American when we vote and choose the people and the laws we wish to live by. It's what makes us willing to fight, to the death if necessary, to defend our freedom and the country we love.

It is our duty to be patriotic towards our country, to stand fast and hard to preserve the "right," and to work hard to correct the "wrongs." To serve our country to the best of our ability, and to defend and keep it safe from our enemies, whoever or whatever they might be.

President John F. Kennedy said: "Ask not what your country can do for you: Ask what you can do for your country."

What can you do for your country? Right now, learning all you can about it's great history, helping other people at all times, obeying laws, being a good citizen, and making your community a better place to live is doing a lot. Think about how you may serve your country in the future.

Show the thousands of men, who gave up their lives for us to be free, that you are proud to be an American.

* Boy Scout Hand Book; sixth printing; 1964; page 399

Week 28
America 4th of July

What does the Fourth of July mean to you? Parades? Fireworks? A day off from school or work? Unfortunately, many of you know very little about the true meaning of the birthday of our country.

On July 4th, 1776, 56 delegates of the Continental Congress, including John Hancock, who was president of the Continental Congress, and Charles Thomsom, who was the Secretary, signed the Declaration of Independence, a document that stated we were no longer willing to be ruled by the British.

The Price They Paid
from the National Federation of National Business

Have you ever wondered what happened to those who signed the Declaration of Independence?

Five signers were captured by the British as traitors, and tortured before they died. Twelve had their homes ransacked and burned. Two lost their sons in the Revolutionary Army, another had two sons captured. Nine of the 56 fought and died from their wounds or the hardships of the Revolutionary War.

What Kind of Men Were They?

Twenty-four were lawyers and jurists. Eleven were merchants, nine were farmers and large plantation owners, men of means, well educated. But they signed the Declaration of Independence knowing full well that the penalty would be death if they were captured. They signed and they pledged their lives, their fortunes, and their sacred honor.

Carter Braxton of Virginia, a wealthy planter and trader, saw his ships swept from the seas by the British navy. He sold his home and properties to pay his debts, and died in rags.

Thomas McKeam was so hounded by the British that he was forced to move his family almost constantly. He served in Congress without pay, and his family was kept in hiding. His possessions were taken from him, and poverty was his reward.

Vandals or soldiers, or both, looted the properties of Heyward, Clymer, Hall, Walton, Gwinnett, Heyward, Rutledge, Ellery, and Middleton.

At the Battle of Yorktown, Thomas Nelson, Jr. noted that the British General Cornwallis, had taken over the Nelson home for his headquarters. The owner quietly urged General George Washington to open fire, which was done. The home was destroyed, and Nelson died bankrupt.

Francis Lewis had his home and his properties destroyed. The enemy jailed his wife, and she died within a few months.

John Hart was driven from his wife's bedside as she was dying. Their 13 children fled for their lives. His fields and his grist mill were laid to waste. For more than a year he lived in forests and caves, returning home after the war to find his wife dead, his children vanished. A few weeks later he died from exhaustion and a broken heart.

Norris and Livingston suffered similar fates.

Such were the stories and sacrifices of the American Revolution. These were not wild-eyed, rabble-rousing ruffians. They were soft spoken men of means and education. They had security, but valued liberty more. Standing tall, straight, and unwavering, they pledged: *"For the support of this Declaration, with firm reliance on the protection of the Divine Providence, we mutually pledge to each other, our lives, our fortunes, and our sacred honor."*

They gave us an Independent America...Can We Keep It?

Week 29
Apathy

Probably one of the biggest problems you face in Scouts today is apathy. Most of you don't even know what the word means, but all of you have been guilty of it, to varying degrees, since you've been a Scout.

Apathy is a lack of interest in a program or event, indifference to whether a program succeeds or fails.

I've seen Scouts say they want to go "here," or do "this or that," and then sit back and expect someone else to do the planning and work to get it done. "Oh my Scoutmaster will handle it" or "I thought so-and-so was going to do that."

Nothing gets done, and the event or program fails. How many campouts or events have failed or come off poorly because of a lack of interest or poor planning since you've been a Scout?

Well it starts with each and every one of you! You are responsible to make sure this program works. This is the "BOY SCOUTS OF AMERICA," Not the "Man" Scouts, not the "Scoutmaster" Scouts, but the BOY SCOUTS! Every Scout in the Troop should have a job, and he should make sure that he's doing that one job to the best of his ability. There's Troop leadership jobs for Senior Patrol Leader, Assistant Senior Patrol Leaders, Quartermaster, Patrol Leaders, Scribe, Historian, Bugler, Librarian, and Chaplain's Aid.

In each of your patrols, you should have an Assist. Patrol Leader, Patrol Quartermaster, Scribe Treasurer, Scribe, Hikemaster, Cheermaster, and Grubmaster.

There is no excuse for anyone in the Troop not to have a job, and they are all important, but only as important as YOU make them. If you don't have a job, talk to your Patrol Leader, Senior Patrol Leader, or Scoutmaster and get one: then find out how to do it, and then do it to the best of your ability. You will make a difference. If everyone in your Patrol did "just that," take the one job and do it to the best of your ability, then your Patrol would be the best it could be

If each Troop Leader did "just that," then your Troop Leadership would be the best it could be, and if each Patrol is performing the best it can, and we have the leaders doing the best they can, then we will have the "Best Troop" around. Then, and only then, will all of your programs succeed! But it has to start with you!

You have to get serious about Scouting. Commit yourself to do the best job you can in whatever job you have, and take it upon yourself to make sure things get done. This is important! Let's start RIGHT NOW! Let's find out if YOU will make a difference.

Week 30
Winning

Everyone loves a winner. And winning is usually a lot more fun than losing. "Winners" aren't usually born that way, though. People who are "winners" have to work hard at it, and you will usually see a lot of practice and dedication from people who win at something. A lot of long hard hours of perfecting their talent or studying their competition, improving their form, or even getting mentally prepared for a competition, goes into a winner's life.

Winning can be more than just being a champion at a sporting event, or being victorious at a competition. You can also be a winner just by using the same techniques they use in their quest to become the best. You can become the "best" at what you want to be, whether it's in Scouts, school, or in your work or play, the basic principals of winning apply.

In whatever your goal is, "practice makes perfect." If you want to be the best at tying knots, you will probably have to tie knots for awhile in order to get good at it. If you want to become a straight "A" student, you will probably have to study what is being taught, and if your goal is to become a sports star, great dancer, singer, or whatever, you will need to set up a time everyday to practice and perfect your talent.

Using these same techniques will help you to become a better Scout as well. If you take what you learn in Scouts, and practice it everyday, you will become better at it. If you study the Scout Law and Promise, you will start to live by it, and if you set aside a time everyday to work at Scouting, whether it be working towards a rank advancement, on a merit badge, or even on next weeks campout, you will become a "winner" in Scouting. And most likely, that winning attitude will also follow you into every other aspect of your life... you will be a winner.

Week 31
Honor

What ever you do, where ever you are, your actions and reactions to the events in your life determine how people feel and think about you. What you do, and how you act will show people what type of person you really are.

Louis IV of France once said "Better a thousand times to die with glory than to live without honor." How can one face themselves if they have no honor? When I've asked you what honor is, some of you have a hard time describing it. Let me put it to you this way. Honorable is the person that you want people to know you as.

If you are the type of person that is known to do what you say you will do, if you care about your family name, and if you want people to know that "your promise" means something, then you are an honorable person.

When you say "On My Honor, I will do my best to do my duty..." your duty is the job or assignment that you have been raised, trained, or have agreed to do.

When you say "To God and My Country" your duty to God is to live by the religious principals that your religion dictates and your duty to your country is to become a good citizen and serve your country to the best of your abilities.

If you can look yourself in the mirror and tell yourself "I am doing my best," then you probably are. In everything you do, you must make a decision... is it right or is it wrong? I'm going to give you a good easy quick "test" to give yourself in making those decisions. This is very important... listen carefully. I call it the "Mommy Test."

When you have to make a decision in life, and you don't know if it's right or wrong, or perhaps you know it's wrong and you think you can "get away" with it... try this. Ask yourself if your mother would be proud of you if you told her what you have done. Would she approve? If the answer is yes, it most likely will be the right decision. If not, then perhaps you better think it over a little more and come up with either the right, or another decision.

Your Honor is everything. The Honor you show in your every day life is how people will judge you.

Week 32
Training

Think of what you have learned so far in Scouting. If you are a Tenderfoot, maybe you've only learned how to tie a square knot or to properly give first aid to someone who needs a bandage. As you progress through the ranks, who will learn how to sharpen and handle a knife and ax, how to safely start a fire, how to read a map and compass, or maybe how to save a life.

The higher you go in Scouting, the more training you receive. The Scouting program serves several purposes, not the least of which is to train young men on how to be prepared.

When Baden-Powell was asked "Be Prepared for what?" he responded "well, Be Prepared for any ol' thing." Don't take your training lightly. You have an opportunity to learn from a program that has been around since 1910; a program that will allow you to learn not only how to take care of yourself, but to be able to take care of others effectively.

Have any of you ever built a model car or plane? It came with instructions, didn't it? Those instructions made the model a little easier to put together, didn't it? Wouldn't it be nice if we had instructions on how to be a teenager or young man? Well guess what? You do!

Your Boy Scout Handbook is probably the best book ever written on how to be a well rounded, intelligent young man. It's chock full of information, and will serve you well in your training as a Scout as well as help you to be prepared for, "well, any ol' thing."

When you get to First Class, ask your Troop leaders about other Training opportunities. We have training courses for Den Chiefs, all the Troop leadership positions, and a week long Junior Leader Training that will offer you insights on effective leadership.

Strive hard to be the best of what you want to be. Take advantage of any and all training you can get. Only in this way will you ever become "Prepared..." "for any ol' thing."

Week 33
Your Uniform

Are you a "Closet Scout?" Are you one of "those Scouts" who will only wear your uniform to a Scout meeting or campout? (and then, only because you have to). Or maybe you'll even wear it during a parade or at a Scout show, but try to hide if you see any of your friends. Most likely you are. In all fairness, you're not alone.

Being a Scout is something in which you can be proud, and obviously, there's something about the program that you like, or else you wouldn't be here. Maybe it's the outdoor adventure, the rank advancement, the fun and excitement of being a leader, or the many different programs that are available to you that keeps your interest.

Whatever the reason, wearing the uniform is part of the program, and those who do wear it correctly should be proud to be seen in it.

During World War II, Baden-Powell told a story of a Scout, who was wearing his Scout uniform. When the German airmen had bombed the train in which he was about to travel, he was at once passed through the police barrier to give help. They recognized that a Scout was not an ordinary boy, but was likely to be useful and helpful; so they passed him through.

He also told of a story about another Scout in uniform who was making his way to the scene of a great explosion. A lady asked him where he was going.

He replied: "To lend a hand with the injured."

"But," said the lady, "you will never get through the police barricade."

"Won't I!" he said. "A fellow who wears his Scout uniform can get anywhere" He was "passed through" all right and did good work for several hours.

So, wearing your Scout uniform can be useful, and also be proud wearing it. But it will also make people expect a great deal from you, so Be Prepared. Train yourself and know what to do in the event of an accident and show that you can do it well for the honor of the Scout Brotherhood. You may be surprised at how many people, your friends included, come up to you and tell you that they were Scouts once, or that they are in Scouting now.

Who knows? Maybe when some of your friends see you in your Scout uniform and find out that you're a Scout, and some of the things that you do in Scouting are pretty exciting, maybe they, too, will want to become a part of your unit.

It only makes sense that if there's something in Scouting that you like, your friends will most likely like it also. What better people to have in your unit then your best friends.

One last thing... if you do wear your Scout uniform, wear it right! Nothing looks worse than someone who wears their uniform sloppily. Be proud of your achievements, of being a Scout, and of wearing the uniform of the Scouting program.

Week 34
Health

One of the best things you can do for yourself is keep yourself in good health. Eating foods that are good for you, exercising regularly, and getting enough sleep will help you to feel your best, keep your mind sharp, and allow you to do many things that other people, who have not maintained their health can't do.

When you are healthy, fit, and strong, you are in control of your body, and can experience many exciting adventures safely.

Scouts are at an age when the temptations of eating too much junk food, drinking a lot of soda, and hitting the "fast food" restaurants, can be a real problem. Only you can control what you eat most of the time, so it's up to you to make the decision to start eating healthy, right now.

Another way many youth effect their health is by the use, or rather misuse of drugs, alcohol, and tobacco. Again, it's up to you too make the decisions on whether you want these things controlling your life. The decisions you make now will effect you not only now, but for the rest of your life.

You are at a time of you life when your body should be the healthiest it will ever be. Go home tonight and look in the mirror. Are you happy with your looks? Do you feel strong and healthy? If the answer is yes, congratulations! If not, sit down and make a plan on how you can get your body in the shape you want it to be.

Write it down! Then start tomorrow on your plan to be a healthier you.

As I've told you many times before, "those who fail to plan, plan to fail..". don't plan to fail yourself on being healthy.

Week 35
Planning

The New Year is a good time to think about planning. It's a time to look back at what has happened during the last year, what you have done, where you have gone, and what you have accomplished. Was it a good Year? Did you do what you wanted to do? Did you reach any of the goals you set for yourself last year? How can you make this year better? Now is the time for you to put into action the plans and resolutions that you've made for this new year. Are you ready?

First of all, have you made any plans or goals? You should have. For your Unit, your Patrol Leaders Council should have already made plans for all of the outings, camping trips, summer camp, and events that you will be doing this year. Have they?

Maybe this is the year you wanted to advance to a higher rank. Have you made any plans on how you are going to achieve that? I have always told the Scouts in my Troop that "those who fail to plan, plan to fail." It's true. If you don't have a plan on what you are going to do, you are planning for failure.

This week, take some time and write down some things you want to do this year. These will be your "short term" goals. Then, next to them, write down some things you would like to do with your life. These will become your "long term" goals, and it's okay if they change later on. Maybe you want to make Eagle Scout this year. Whatever it is that you want to accomplish, write it down. Then, start making plans on how you can achieve those goals. Do it this week... start making plans to succeed now.

Week 36
Hazing

Have you ever played a joke on someone, maybe an innocent little prank just to have some fun? Most of us have, and most of the time, as long as it doesn't hurt anyone or put someone in danger, it's not really a problem. But then there are the times that are a problem, and that's what we need to talk about now.

Remember back when you first joined the Scouts? There was a group of new Scouts that you had met for the first time, and you probably didn't feel like "one of the gang" yet. That is normal. It happens to all of us at one time or the other, and if someone compounds that uneasiness with some sort of prank or initiation, that is what is called "hazing," and is not good.

Hazing can also be calling someone by a derogatory nickname that he doesn't like, or intentionally ignoring or avoiding a Scout because you don't like him. These types of actions do not portray the Scout Oath and Law, and are not acceptable.

We must always strive to make our friends and fellow Scouts welcome, and part of the group. The better we all feel about the people in our Unit, the better the Unit is going to be. The better someone feels about the Scouts they have around them, the better Scouts they will be.

The "Golden Rule" comes to mind when I talk about hazing: "Do unto others as you would have them do unto you."

Don't be the cause of someone leaving because you didn't make them feel welcome. Strive to be the friendliest Scout in the group.

Share your knowledge, experiences, and Scout "know-how" with all the new Scouts. Help make your unit the "best" it can be by making it the "Friendliest" it can be. You can and do make a difference!

Week 37
Ambition

There's an old German proverb that states "Every eel hopes to become a whale." We all dream of what it would be like to be rich and famous, own a fancy car, or travel the world. There's nothing wrong with working hard to better yourself, or to set a goal and work hard to achieve it. Ambition is that desire you have to achieve whatever it is that you want. A strong desire to gain wealth, prestige, or power through leadership is healthy as long as it's legal and doesn't hurt someone.

The first thing an ambitious person must do is decide what it is they want to put all of their efforts into. Your present goal may be to achieve Eagle Scout, or maybe to become a first string player on your schools football or basketball team. What ever it is, you show your ambition by the amount of effort you put into the goal.

If you don't work hard, and seek out help in your advancement in Scouting, or never attend practice or work out for your sport, you lack ambition, at least in the achievement of these goals. But if you are the kind of Scout who is always seeking out ways to get things signed off in your Scout Handbook for advancement, or are constantly exercising and working out so that you are in the best physical shape you can be for the sport you choose, your efforts will be noticed, you will become known as an ambitious person, and you will succeed. You will also be developing personal and work ethics along the way that will stay with you for the rest of your life.

Yes, the drive, determination, and courage to achieve the goals you set for yourself will measure the ambition you will be known by. Your experience in the many Scouting programs will help give you the knowledge and skills that you will need to fulfill your choices.

Make your choices carefully, choose the Scouting programs, school courses, and personal leisure time activities that will best suite the achievement of these goals.

Week 38
Conservation

One of the most important issues to surface today is the conservation of our world resources. How many of you recycle everything that you can at home? Most of you probably recycle soda cans, mostly because you can get money for them. And some of you may even save newspapers and glass. Did you know you can get money for them too? But what about some of the other things we use everyday? What about plastic soda jugs, or cardboard milk cartons? How long a shower do you take? Do you let the water run down the gutters when you water your lawn or trees and shrubs? Does your toilets and shower heads have water conservation control devices installed? Then there is the electricity we use in the house... do you leave your lights on when you leave a room? Does your Mom use the clothes dryer when she can hang your clothes out to dry? Is your thermostat set at 68 degrees? Do you leave your heater or air conditioner on when nobody is home?

These are all things we can do to not only save money at home, but to also help save some of our resources. We must all work very hard at recycling everything we can so as to not destroy our environment. Everyone of you can make a difference! But we must all work together, individually, as a family, as a troop, as a community, and as a nation to conserve our resources and reuse all that we can. Recycling and conservation isn't just a "fad," it's our guarantee that we will have a world for our future generations.

Week 39
Courage

Courage can take many forms, but true courage is to stand up for what you believe in, be willing, if necessary, to fight for it, and to stand by your decisions.

You are faced with many tough decisions today. Peer pressure from your friends, school mates, and in many cases, gangs of people who may test your courage to do what you believe is right. It may be very difficult for you at times, and only you can muster up the courage to deal with it when the time comes. That is when true men of courage show their bravery, grit, and guts.

To face someone who is offering you drugs or alcohol and telling them "NO!" takes guts.

To tell someone that they are wrong to drink, or take drugs, even though they may be a friend of yours, shows grit.

To stand up against a gang or group that is trying to make you do something you don't believe in shows bravery.

And then to do something about it, to help them or see that they get help takes true courage. This type of courage is the mark of true friendship and will brand you not only as a valued friend, but as a courageous and good man.

Think about the people you know, the friends you have, or maybe even a member of your family. Is there someone you know who may be headed down the wrong road in life. How can you help? What can you do to help them get back on the right road?

How much courage can you muster up to help the people who mean the most to you... only you can answer these questions.

Week 40
Danger

There is danger in almost everything we do in life. If you don't look both ways when crossing the street, there is a danger that you could be hit by a car. If you don't put your money in a safe spot, there's a danger someone could take it, or if you are not prepared, your next campout could become dangerous.

There are many kinds of dangers, and for the most part, you learn about the dangers around your house, and how to avoid them from your parents, school, and friends. But when you go out into the outdoors though, there's a whole new set of dangers to be concerned with, dangers that your parents and friends may not know about, and dangers that are not normally taught in school.

Animals, poisonous plants and insects, the terrain, and even the weather can pose many dangers that you will need to know about when going out into the great outdoors to survive. Some people are afraid of snakes, spiders, bears, or a variety of other things that they will find when going camping or hiking. You must learn about and respect these things in the outdoors in order to be safe. Just like your parents telling you to look both ways when crossing the street, your Scouting can show you what poison oak or poison sumac looks like.

You can learn how to prepare for and hike and camp in bad weather. You can learn how to respect the wild animals in your area while you are visiting in their "home." You can learn to face and deal with these dangers in a safe way by becoming knowledge able about them. You can conquer your fears by learning how to respect and know the dangers surrounding them. The more you learn, the safer you will be when facing danger.

Week 41
Forgetfulness

How many times have you gone on a camping trip when someone has forgotten something? For most of us, it's almost every time. It may have been your canteen, your knife, or mess kit. Or maybe even the food for your patrol. We all have "stories" to tell when someone has forgotten something. If it's just something that effects you, it's usually not too bad, but if it's something that effects your whole patrol or troop, then it can be quite embarrassing.

What about forgetting other things like the Outdoor Code, or the Scout law? These are things that you may have learned once, and because you do not use them, they get forgotten. That's the way it is with most things that people forget.

If they don't use or see it often, they forget about it. Sometimes we just need to look in the book once in awhile and keep these things "fresh" in our minds. By looking at them once in a while, it will help to remind us of how we are to remember to use them in our lives.

I remember a young Scout once who was asked to sing his favorite song at a camporee campfire, and even though he knew the song quite well, wound up forgetting some of the words half way into the song. Needless to say, he was quite embarrassed, and since then, always takes the words with him on a piece of paper in case he forgets.

There is nothing wrong with making notes to yourself in order to help you remember things. Most successful business men carry a "daily reminder" calendar or notebook with them everyday to help them to remember things. Most successful Scouts take good notes as well, and learn to rely on these notes when it's time to put them into action.

If you have a problem forgetting things, or remembering things for that matter, try carrying a small notebook with you to help you. Write down the things you need to take on a campout and refer to them when you go. Write down the things you have trouble remembering, and look at it each day until it's memorized. And write down important dates and events so that you will know what's coming up and how to plan for them.

These things will help you to be known as the Scout who remembers everything, not the Scout who forgets everything.

Week 42
Forgiveness

Have you ever hurt a friend, or forgotten to do something you were supposed to do? Were you ever caught telling a lie, or taking something that you weren't supposed to take? Most likely all of us have been guilty of something like this sometime in our lives, and hopefully, have been forgiven for it, by either saying we were sorry or promising not to do it again, or perhaps by being punished for the act and suffering the consequences.

But let's turn it around. Can you think of someone who has lied to you or stolen from you? Do you remember how you felt? Do you still harbor bad feelings and resentfulness toward this person? We are all human and make mistakes once in awhile. You must find it in your heart to try and understand why this person did what they did, and to help them to understand that it is not proper behavior.

Just to forgive them is not enough, you must also consider taking action on why they did what they did, and insure that it doesn't happen again.   You will find it easier to forgive and help those who have done something wrong to you than to harbor ill feelings and let it bother you for the rest of your life. Bringing the matter out in the open with an honest, straight forward, approach will usually bring it to a amiable solution.

Giving the person a "way out," will usually create a new and sincere bond that may lead to a stronger friendship. But most importantly, you will not be carrying around all those bad feelings and hatred that will fester and grow in you when you don't forgive someone for something. Learn to forgive, and then, forget it. You will be a much happier person for it in the long run.

Week 43
Freedom

One of the greatest treasures you have is your freedom. Most of you do not know the price that has been paid for you to be a free person, but know it well that the fight for freedom has been a long battle with thousands of our forefathers giving their lives to keep it. Learn all you can in your history classes about how they fought to keep our freedom.

Let's think about something real quick. How would you feel if tomorrow, another country took over the United States, and said that you must now stay in your own city. If you want to cross the county line, you will need a permit, and that would be almost impossible to get.

Now let's say that this new country tells your parents that any boy over the age of 14 must join their army and fight for them, usually without much training, to preserve the better trained soldiers from their country. Oh yes, and your family would now be put on rations. You won't be allowed to go to the store until a certain day and even then, you may not get all the food you need. They may even come and take your car, or limit gasoline to certain people. The only TV you can watch is whatever the government wants you to watch, and all movies will either be censored or banned by the government. You would have no control over how the government spent your money or raised your taxes.

Hmmmmm... does that sound like some place you would want to live? There are countries in this world that do live like that, and unless we protect our freedom, we could be that way too. A country only deserves the amount of freedom it is willing to defend and fight for. All of the wars our country has fought has been for the preservation of our basic freedoms and the right of people to be free everywhere. You choice to choose is a priceless inheritance.

The best thing you can do right now to help preserve the freedom in our country is to learn all you can about how we've fought to keep it, and how we will fight to keep from losing it. Learn how our government works, and how important it is to vote, not only for the best people to put in office, but for the best laws to run our country.

Learn about our country, talk about issues that are important, and then do what you can to change what is wrong and preserve the freedom we've come to live by.

Week 44
Habits

Some of you bite your fingernails, some of you have a little saying like "cool" or "that's fresh" or something else that you always say. Other's eat the same cereal everyday or have the same type of sandwich for lunch all the time. These are all habits, some good, some bad, and some, well, some are just habits.

Let's talk about some "bad" habits that some of you might have, and maybe don't even know about. How many people do you know that are always "cutting someone down" or saying bad things about people? How about the Scout who is always bullying someone or "putting them down."

These are also examples of reoccurring behavior that could be construed as habits. These types of people usually need help even to recognize that there is a problem. If you know of someone who does these things, maybe you can help by mentioning that they may be hurting peoples feelings by saying these things and that they should try to be more friendly.

What about the Scouts who have a "smoking" or "drinking" habit? Or even drugs! These are also people who may need help to break these habits, help that even you, as their friend, may not be able to give them. Maybe you can help them to seek professional help to help break these habits.

Then there are the "good" habits that we should all strive to make a part of our everyday lives. Getting up on time, eating right, getting enough exercise. Making and keeping a time to do your chores and homework, or studies and getting to bed on time. By making these things important, practicing them everyday, we will make these our good habits that will stay with us for life. I've heard it said that if you make a conscience effort to make or break a habit for 39 days, and stick to it, it will be yours for life. Try this out for any habits you want to make or break, and let's try to make all of our habits good ones.

Week 45
Imagination

One of my heroes as a youth was Walt Disney, a man with one of the greatest imaginations of the twentieth century. A man who brought us Mickey Mouse, Donald Duck, incredible animated motion pictures, Disneyland, and the EPCOT Center/ Disney World Complex in Florida. Things weren't always great for Walt Disney, but by sticking to his dreams, and using his imagination to stir all kinds of feelings in people all over the world, he was able to build an empire of fun and exciting dreams for people of all ages.

You too can use your imagination to create new and exciting adventures and events for the people around you. Think of new and exciting ways for the Scouts in your patrol and troop to learn about Scouting while having fun doing it. Think up new games that you can play that will teach some of the things we do in Scouting. Use your imagination to create new skits and songs for campfires and Scout Shows.

Your dreams are only limited by your imagination. Making your dreams into a reality will take concentration, some common sense, and a lot of imagination. Only you will put the limits on those efforts. Use your imagination to set your goals, find solutions, and achieve your dreams. Imagine yourself succeeding in these dreams and you will.

Week 46
Jealousy

Sometimes you have a friend who does better than you at something and it makes you angry. Perhaps they have studied harder or practiced more, or maybe are just in better shape than you. You must not be jealous of their achievements though, or you might wind up losing their friendship. Everyone should always strive to do their best. You should be happy for those who beat you for doing their best, and work harder yourself, next time, so that you will do better. If they "let you" win, that would be an empty victory, something that you would not feel very good about.

Jealousy is when you feel threatened by someone else who may be trying to take something from you. It could be a "title" in a sporting event, a position in a club or team, or even a girlfriend. In the case of a sporting event, the "best" should always win... that's what sports is all about.

This holds true for people seeking an office or position, the best person for the job should get it. You may not agree with the choice, but being honest and forthright about it is usually the best way to handle it.

In matters of girlfriends, being honest and direct, is usually the best way to bring the best results, that, and the confidence and attention that normally goes along with matters of romance.

In any case, being jealous of someone should stop short of losing them as a friend, and go just far enough to spark that flame in yourself to do better.

Don't let jealousy become so bad in you that you start doing stupid things. It is important that you maintain control of you actions at all times. Letting jealousy get the better of you will make you blind to common sense and will seldom achieve the results you want. Be strong, and confident, and the need for jealousy will seldom bear it's ugly head... and you will be known as the better person for it.

Week 47
Knowledge

What do you know? A lot of things! And everyday you learn something new... but how do you use the knowledge you've gained? Is the knowledge you learn useful, or is it just something that stays in the back of your head waiting to be forgotten. So now, we have to take a look at the different types of knowledge that people learn.

Most of you are probably pretty good at video or computer games. You may have gained the "knowledge" of how to solve the games, or where certain secret passages are in the games, but does that knowledge really help you in everyday life? Probably not. Even though video games probably help in developing your hand-eye coordination, and may have some recreational value, this knowledge will seldom help develop your career or scholastic endeavors.

Then there's the knowledge that is taught to you in school. Math, history, English, and the other subjects that you take are designed to help you not only now, but in the future. This type of knowledge is important, and must be learned if you are to be successful in life. The knowledge learned in school will benefit you for the rest of your life, and will determine what you can, or cannot do for a living when you graduate.

Finally, there's the knowledge you learn from your experiences and "outside" activities such as sports, clubs, and Scouts. The knowledge you obtain from these types of activities will help "round out" your education to make you more aware of the world around you and better informed to the problems that face it. Knowledge about the environment, your community, how to survive in the outdoors, how to camp, fish, hike, or live off the land are all important bits of knowledge that will allow you to enjoy and preserve the world around you. Take learning seriously. Plant the seeds of knowledge early, continuously feed it, care for it, and rely on it so that it will take care of you when you need it the most.

Week 48
Love

There is a feeling, a power, a source of emotion within us all that is so strong, so powerful that entire wars have been fought over and about it. More words have been written about it than any other word in history, and no matter what sex, race, religion, or belief you are, everyone has felt it.

When asked to explain it, most of you will smile, some will be a little embarrassed, but all will have trouble defining it, as do most people... but we all have experienced it in one form or another.

Love is a very complex emotion or feeling that can take on many forms. You love your Mom, Dad, and family. You love God. You love your home, or perhaps your school, or maybe the city that you live in. You may "love" ice cream, playing video games or being on the baseball or football team. You may have a special friend that you love, or a best friend that you love to be around. You may love to go hiking, camping, and swimming, or just being in the outdoors. As I said, love can mean many things.

There is one thing that almost any type of love means to most people, it's that they care about that which they love. They want to protect it, keep it from harm, and watch it grow. Love is all around us and the more love we give, the more we receive, and the happier we are.

I hope you all acquire a love of Scouting as I have. I love to see all of you learn about Scouting, and enjoy the many adventures and opportunities it offers. I love to see you all learn how to live in the outdoors, how it builds your character, and how you learn about citizenship in our great country. I love the way it encourages you to become physically fit, and morally straight. But most of all, I love the way it shows all of you how to become good, strong, young men with great values.

Week 49
Leadership

Dwight D. Eisenhower, the 34th President of the United States once said that "Leadership is the art of getting someone else to do something you want done because he wants to do it."

There are many styles of leadership, and you have probably seen a few of them here in your unit. Maybe you've been to a Junior Leadership Course, or have served as one of your units leaders. Who are the best leaders in your unit?

Most of you probably already know that being a leader isn't always easy, and sometimes you have to make tough decisions. The best leaders are those of you who manage to get the job done by making sure everyone helps and has something to do. Delegating different parts of the job to those who are best suited to complete the task makes it fun for everyone and usually makes for a better job.

Are you one of the leaders in your unit? Do you want to be? Being a leader means taking on the duties of the position you want, as well as accepting responsibility for both the successes and the failures. But there is no better feeling than that of a leader who has gained the respect and trust of the people he leads. When a leader gets the people he's in charge of working together as a team, having fun, and "getting the job done because they want to do it," then that's the mark of a good leader.

There are many leadership positions available to you as a Scout. Talk to your unit leaders and ask what is available. Take the time to learn how to do the job you have selected to the best of your ability, select and train the people you lead how they can best help you, and make the job fun. Soon you too will be known as a "Good Leader."

Week 50
Romance

Most of you may have the wrong definition in mind when we talk about romance. If you look in the dictionary, romance is defined as "adventurous, heroic, or picturesque character or nature, strange and fascinating appeal, the disposition to delight in mysterious adventures"

All of these definitions describe some part of the Scouting program or events that you have been, or will be involved in. Scouting is unique in that it offers such a diverse and varied program. It offers to solve some of the mysteries of nature by giving first hand knowledge and experience in the outdoors. It provides you with adventure by letting you decide when and where you want to go hiking, camping, or exploring. And as you get older, the program is designed to make the adventures more exciting and challenging.

Romance is the excitement you feel when you've climbed your first mountain, see your first deer up close, or rappel 200 feet down into a cave. Romance is the adventure you live when you do your first 50 mile hike through the wilderness, spend a week at a high adventure camp, or go on a National Jamboree tour with 40,000 other Scouts. Romance is the pride and respect you achieve when you've earned the highest rank in The Boy Scouts of America, your Eagle Scout Award.

The "strange and fascinating appeal" that the Scouting program offers has been attracting young men like yourself since 1910. The romance you will experience in Scouting will certainly give birth to many "loves" in your life... a love of nature, a love of friends, and a love of the world around you being just a few of them.

So, when you think of "romance," give a quick thought to the adventure, excitement, and pride you've experienced in Scouting, and remember, like most things in life, you only get out of it what you put into it.

Week 51
Becoming A Young Man

Is becoming a young man difficult? Well, some of you handle it better than others, and some of you think your handling it pretty good, or at least your trying to convince everyone that you are. But in reality, most of you all will have at least some problems dealing with growing up. It's how you deal with these problems that will decide what kind of a man you will be.

The problems that come up most for young men your age are girls, sports, and cars. "Will that girl think I'm cool if she finds out I'm a Boy Scout? How can I do all those things in Scouts when I need to go to practice everyday? The Coach will kick me off the team if I don't show up. I can't go on that camp-out, I have to work. I have to have money for gas and insurance for my car." Sound familiar?

These are the same problems that have been facing young men your age for years. You have some important decisions to make, and only YOU can make them.

Having a girlfriend can be a fun and exciting time for a young man. And having a young lady around doesn't mean you have to give up everything else. Remember, she liked the Scout you were when she met you, and that included all of the things you were involved in at the time.

You should start out your relationship with honesty and respect for each other, only in that way will it ever grow stronger. Having a car, or a job is another type of responsibility you will be, or are facing.

Again, you should take on only that which is important to you, and keep your goals in sight. It will be up to you to keep on track in achieving those goals.

You aren't alone though. You have your parents and family, your religious leaders, and your adult Scout Leaders who are all willing to talk and help if you need it. You also have a "manual" on how to act and react to a bunch of things you might run into. A book on how to be a good man, a good citizen, and a great Scout, Your Boy Scout Handbook! When's the last time you actually read it? And then, of course, there's another great book that can help as well... your Bible. It's a great book. You should pick it up and read it sometime. All these people and things are right there, waiting to help you if you need it; to help you make and achieve the goals you have set for yourself.

Yes, becoming a young man can be scary, but it can also be exciting, adventurous, and fulfilling if you follow the basic ethics laid out in the Scout Oath and Law. You are in the best youth program in the world! It will lead you down the trail to manhood and good living.

Week 52
B.P.'s Last Message To Boy Scouts

Dear Scouts:

If you have ever seen the play, Peter Pan, you will remember how the pirate chief was always making his dying speech, because he was afraid that possibly, when the time came for him to die, he might not have time to get it off his chest.

It is much the same with me; and so, although I am not at this moment dying, I shall be doing so one of these days, and I want to send you a parting word of good goodbye.

Remember it is the last you will ever hear from me, so think it over.

I have had a most happy life, and I want each one of you to have as happy a life too.

I believe that God put us in this jolly world to be happy and enjoy life. Happiness doesn't come from being rich, nor merely from being successful in your career, nor by self indulgence. One step towards happiness is to make yourself healthy and strong while you are a boy, so that you can be useful, and so can enjoy life when you are a man.

Nature study will show you how full of beautiful and wonderful things God has made the world for you to enjoy. Be contented with what you have got, and make the best of it; look on the bright side of things instead of the gloomy one.

But the real way to get happiness is by giving out happiness to other people. Try and leave this world a little better than you found it, And when your turn comes to die you can die happy in feeling that at any rate you have not wasted your time but have done your best.

'Be Prepared' in this way, to live happy and to die happy; stick to your Scout Promise always even after you have ceased to be a boy and God help you do it.

Your friend,
Baden-Powell of Gilwell

CHAPTER

2

12 Monthly Religious Minutes

Month 1
Beginnings
A New Year

The New Year always brings to mind what I have done or accomplished during the last year. I write down my "new years resolutions" making them my written goals for the year, and then look at them the following year to see if I've accomplished any of my objectives or to see how my goals have changed. The new year is full of mystery and romance, it's a time for dreams and planned and unplanned adventures... a time of renewal an betterment. It is a time to thank God for the many wonders and gifts he has provided for us during the last year.

What plans have you made for the year to come. How do you plan to make these plans a reality. What have you done to make sure you and your patrol or troop will have a year of great adventures and excitement.

I have always live by the premise that "Those who fail to plan, plan to fail." If you don't plan to have fun, adventures, and excitement, it's a good chance you won't. Make sure your patrol or troop have made good plans for the upcoming year, write them down as goals, and next year, look at them and see if you've succeeded. Then pray that God will give you the strength, wisdom and courage to make them a reality.

Take time tonight and try to remember what you have seen and done during the last year. How has Scouting touched your lives? How can you make a difference this coming year? Each and every one of you has the potential to make a big difference in your patrol and troop, and for that matter, in our world.

Pray to God that you have a safe and wonderful year, and that with his guidance, this will be the best year of your life. Start by making a point of helping your patrol or troop to achieve the plans you have made for the year, and then, most importantly, have fun and thank God everyday for his support, love, and guidance.

Month 2
Scout's Own Service
(In The Woods)

Look around you. Listen to the wind, the birds in the trees, and the sound of nature all around us. That is God's voice speaking to us and welcoming us into his magnificent home.

Some of us worship in churches, synagogues, or holy places each week, but today we are here in the splendor of the outdoors visiting our Lord in his garden. What better place to "get close to our God" than in that which he has given us to enjoy.

With that being said, I now offer these excerpts from the 104th Psalms:

> *Bless the Lord, O my soul!*
> *O Lord, my God, you are great indeed!*
>
> *You have constructed your palace upon the waters.*
> *You make the clouds your chariot.*
>
> *You travel on the wings of the wind.*
> *You make the winds your messengers*
> *and flaming fire your ministers.*
>
> *You send forth springs into the watercourses,*
> *And wind among the mountains,*
> *And gave drink to every beast in the field,*
> *till the wild beast's quench their thirst.*
>
> *Beside them the birds of the heavens dwell;*
> *from among the branches they send forth their song.*
> *You water the mountains from your palace;*
> *the earth is replete with the fruit of your works.*
>
> *You raise grass for the cattle,*
> *and vegetation for men's use,*
> *producing bread from the earth,*
> *and wine to gladden men's hearts.*

May the glory of the Lord endure forever;
may the Lord be glad in his works!

I will sing to the Lord all my life;
I will sing praise to my God while I live.
Amen *

As you walk in the outdoors today, look around at the many splendors around you, be happy to be here and enjoy what you see. Thank God for his many miracles. Go in Peace, and may God Bless and keep you safe.

Footnote:
Taken in part from the 1990 BSA statement on God in Scouting.

Month 3
Time to Pray

I got up early one morning
and rushed right into the day.
I had so much to accomplish
that I didn't take time to pray.

Problems just tumbled about me,
and heavier came each task.
"Why doesn't God Help me?," I wondered.
He answered, "You didn't ask."

I wanted to see joy and beauty,
but the day toiled on, gray and bleak.
I wondered why God didn't show me,
He said, "But you didn't seek,"

I tried to come into God's presence.
I used all my keys at the lock.
God gently and lovingly chided,
"My child you didn't knock."

I woke up early this morning,
and paused before entering the day.
I had so much to accomplish
that I had to take time to pray.

(Author Unknown)

Month 4
A Scout Prayer

Great Master of all good Scouts, we pray that Thou will make us trustworthy, for those are they who trust us. Make us loyal, for through loyalty we reach our highest ideals.

Teach us to be helpful, through helpfulness we remember others first and are remembered for our good deeds.

Make us friendly, there are many who need our friendship. Make us kind, the fields and woods are full of thy creatures. Insist upon our obedience, for success comes only to him who first learns to obey.

Make us cheerful, for cheerfulness is like green grass under your bare feet or the water that dances in the stream. Train us in thrift, for thrifty habits enable us to be generous to those in need.

May we be brave, brave in darkness and brave in light, but save us from becoming fakers of bravery.

Help us to be clean, in thought, in speech, and in deed; and may we remember that our bodies are Thy holy temple.

Above all, Great Master, help us to be reverent, not only toward Thee but toward all things that Thou hast made.

We ask Thy guidance in all things... and may we never forget the Promise to which all Scouts are pledged.

Amen

Month 5
Prayer

One of the things that most of us have done, ever since we were old enough to talk, is pray. Maybe it started when you were going to bed with a little bedtime prayer like "Now I lay me down to sleep, I pray the Lord my soul to keep, if I should die before I wake, I pray the Lord my soul to take." Maybe you added a "God Bless Mom and Dad, your sisters and brothers," and such. The important thing was that you were learning an important and very powerful lesson. How to make praying to God an everyday event, one that can change your life.

Now maybe it's been a little while sense you've prayed to God, and that's OK. But wouldn't it nice to know there was always someone there to talk **to**? Someone you know could help?

If you think of God as a friend, instead of something some Scout is "talking about" at church, then you can start talking to this friend about your problems, and asking him if he can help. Guess what, that's what praying is. And it works!

Praying to God helps you "talk out" your problems with the one who can help you the most. You! With God's guidance and help, you can solve any problem. And sometimes, it's OK just to say "hi" to God, maybe as you pass your church, or say "thank you" to God when something nice happens.

Reinhold Niebuhr wrote a great little verse called the "Serenity Prayer" that has been used by millions of people around the world. Maybe you could use it too, as a way of starting your daily talks with God. It goes like this:

"God grant me the Serenity to accept the things I cannot change, the courage to change the things I can, and the wisdom to know the difference"

Use this, or a verse of your own choosing, and say hello to God at least once a day. And as with all good friends, I'm sure he will appreciate it if you come visit him once a week as well. The important thing though, is to know that you can talk to God and know that he is listening. That's what prayer is all about.

NOTE: *(Pass out copies of the Prayer to all of the participants)*

Month 6
Sermons We See

by Edgar A. Guest

I'd rather see a sermon than to hear one any day;
I'd rather one should walk with me than merely tell the way.
The eye's a better pupil and more willing than the ear;
Fine council is confusing, but example's always clear;
And the best of all the preachers are the men who live their creeds,
For to see good put in action is what everybody needs.

I soon can learn to do it if you'll let me see it done;
I can watch your hands in action, but your tongue too fast may run.
And the lecture you deliver may be very wise and true;
But I'd rather get my lessons by observing what you do.
For I might misunderstand you and the high advice you give,
But there's no misunderstanding how you act and how you live.

When I see a deed of kindness, I am eager to be kind.
When a weaker brother stumbles and a strong man stays behind
Just to see if he can help him, then the wish grows strong in me,
To become as big and thoughtful as I know that I can be.
And all the travelers can witness that the best of guides today
Is not the one who tells you, but the one who shows the way.

One good man teaches many, men believe what they behold;
One deed of kindness noticed is worth forty that are told.
Who stands with men of honor learns to hold his honor dear,
For right living speaks a language which to everyone is clear.
Though an able speaker charms me with his eloquence, I say,
I'd rather see a sermon than to hear one, any day.

Month 7
Belief

An anonymous old verse says:
I believe in the sun – even when it doesn't shine;
I believe in love – even when it is not shown;
And I believe in God, even when He does not speak.

Sometimes it is hard to believe in something that you cannot see, hear, touch, or smell. But that does not mean it is not real. When I was a young man, I, like most of you will, fell in love with a beautiful lady, and wanted to marry her. But, it was not to be, and we parted. I could not see the love or the hurt, I could not smell it, nor could I taste or touch it, but I certainly felt it with all of my heart. Later, when I fell in love again, and did marry, I again felt the love and the feelings that could not be heard or seen. They were certainly real!

When I started learning of God as a young man, I only knew that there was a lot of people who went to a place once a week and talked about a man who lived long ago. Someone on his birthday we received a lot of presents, and who's death and Resurrection at Easter got our family together. Someone who was not "alive" now, but was still with us.

And as time passed, I started to "feel" his presence, I started to know this man, and respect his wishes. I still cannot see him, nor touch or smell him, but I certainly can feel him with me everyday, and know that it is He that I must answer to in my actions, in what I do, and in what I fail to do.

We all believe in someone or something. Not to believe would mean that we would cease to exist. My belief in God keeps me strong, keeps me on the right path, and guides me in my journey though life. My love of life, and God, and belief in love, keeps me happy and contented. The power of God is there, yours for the asking... it's up to you to ask.

Month 8
Twelve Guidelines for Living

A Biblical Perspective on the Scout Law
(author unknown)

In 1911, The Official Handbook for Boys was published by the then fledgling Boy Scouts of America. This book presented to Americans an organization with a framework of duty to God and country and a cornerstone of unselfish service to mankind. The strength and authority of this great organization was to be a firm foundation called the Scout Law.

In the more than 80 years since the Official Handbook for Boys went to press, Scouting has kept pace with modern approaches while broadening its scope. Yet the foundation remains firm, offering to today's youth the same moral guidance espoused in 1911.

Upon studying the 12 points of the Scout Law, you can quickly recognize a well-balanced guide for living. Each of these 12 points find positive support from the pages of the Holy Bible. As evidence of this biblical support a sampling of passages is provided.

I. A SCOUT IS TRUSTWORTHY – I CORINTHIANS 4:1-2
    (NASV): "Let a man regard us in this manner, as servants of Christ, and stewards of the mysteries of God. In this case, moreover, it is required of stewards that one be found trustworthy."

II. A SCOUT IS LOYAL – PROVERBS 19:22A (RSV):
    "What is desired in a man is loyalty."

III. A SCOUT IS HELPFUL – MATTHEW 25:35-36 (KJV):
    "For I was hungered, and ye gave me meat:
    I was thirsty, and ye gave me drink:
    I was a stranger and ye took me in:
    Naked and ye clothed me:
    I was sick and ye visited me:
    I was in prison, and ye came unto me."

PROVERBS (MOFFATT):
"Never refuse help to your neighbor, when you can render it."

IV.   A Scout is Friendly – John 15:12-13 (NASV):
      Jesus said, "This is my commandment, that you love on another just as
      I have loved you. Greater love has no one than this, that one lay
      down his life for his friends."

V.   A Scout is Courteous – I Peter 3:8 (KJV)
      "Finally, be ye all of one mind, having compassion of one another, love
      as brethren, be pitiful, be courteous."

VI.   A Scout is Kind – Ephesians 4:32 (NASV):
      "And be kind to on another, tender-hearted, forgiving each other just
      as God in Christ also has forgiven you."

VII. A Scout is Obedient – Hebrews 13:17a (NASV):
      "Obey your leaders and submit to them for they keep watch over your
      souls, as those who will give account."

Ephesians 6:1 (NASV)
      "Children, obey your parents in the Lord, for this is right."

VIII. A Scout is Cheerful – Proverbs 17:22a (RSV):
      "A cheerful heart is good medicine."

IX.   A Scout is Thrifty – Romans 12:10-11 (NASV):
      "The thoughts of the diligent tend only to plenteousness."

X.   A Scout is Brave – II Timothy 1:7 (NASV):
      "For God has not given us a spirit of timidity but of   power and love
      and discipline."

XI.   A Scout is Clean – Psalm 51:10 (NASV):
      Create in me a clean heart, O God, and renew a right spirit within me."

XII. A Scout is Reverent – Proverbs 19:23 (LB):
      "Reverence for God gives life, happiness, and protection from harm."

Psalm 34:9 (Moffatt):
      "Revere the Eternal, O ye saints of his, the reverent never want for any-
      thing."

Month 9
Footprints

We must obey God rather than men.

– Acts 5:29

In what ever you do, where ever you go, God is watching you. God will be there when you need him, and will help and guide you though your troubled times. Some of you may be familiar with the story called "FOOTPRINTS' from an unknown author." It is one of my favorites, listen carefully:

Footprints

"One night a man had a dream. He dreamed he was walking along the beach with the Lord. Across the sky flashed scenes from his life. For each scene he noticed two sets of footprints in the sand; one belonging to him, and the other to the Lord.

When the last scene of his life flashed before him, he looked back at the footprints in the sand. He noticed that many times along the path of his life there was only one set of footprints. He also noticed that this happened at the very lowest, and saddest times in his life.

This really bothered him and he questioned the Lord about it. "Lord, you said that once I decided to follow you, you'd walk with me all the way. But I have noticed that during the most troublesome times in my life, there is only one set of footprints in the sand. I don't understand why, when I needed you most, you would leave me."

The Lord replied: "My son, my precious child, I love you and would never leave you. During your times of trial and suffering, when you see only one set of footprints, it was then that I carried you."

Believe in the Lord, let him guide you and lead the way. Let him "Carry" you when you are down, and remember to walk in His footprints... He has left them there for you to follow.

Month 10
A Friend of Mine

Let me tell you about a friend of mine. He is very interested in you and I. He has always been there to help you and me and is watching us all the time. As a matter of fact, I was talking with Him the other day and He told me that He had been watching you as you were walking with some of your friends and was a little sad that you hadn't said hello to Him that day. He waited all day long, and even though He was there, you never stopped to chat.

Later that evening, after He had given us a sensational sunset and a nice cool breeze to help us end our day, you again forgot all about Him. But He said it was okay, and that He still loves you because He is your friend too.

He saw you fall asleep, and longed to be in your dreams. He wanted you to have a peaceful night so He gave you soft moonlight and shiny stars to help calm you and put you into a restful sleep. He was there again when you woke, and hoped to hear from you, to have you ask Him for another great day, to pray that you will be kept from harm. He has so many things to tell you and so much to give.

And that day, not too long ago, when you woke up late and rushed off into the day, things were going so badly for you and He really wanted to help, but you never asked. And when your best friend let you down, and hurt you, He understood that too. His tears were the rain that was falling that day, but again, He said it was okay, and that He understood. People disappoint Him everyday too, but He still loves them.

He has tried to talk to you in the mountains; the wind, leaves, and water shouting His messages at you, but you didn't listen. The birds sing His songs and the gentle breeze quietly whispers His love for you. His love surrounds us all, and is there, just for the asking.... but you do have to ask.

Yes, I want to tell you about my friend, His name is Jesus, and He would like me to tell you that He's there, anytime you want, to help you and guide you through your life. All you have to do is visit Him once in a while, say hello, and ask for His help... oh, some people call that "praying," I call it talking to my best friend.

Month 11
Miwok Indian Dance of Thanks

The Miwok Indians of Central California were a peaceful people who were the ultimate conservationists. They only took from the land what they needed, used everything they took, and gave thanks for the many blessings they had.

One of the ways they gave thanks was in the form of a dance that they did in a "Round House," a special underground structure that served as a religious assembly area for them.

They formed a circle around a campfire with four members representing the four seasons, and four members representing the four points of the compass. They rotated around the campfire representing the changing seasons. They also had two other members who represented the sun and the moon, two very important things in the lives of these Indians, who revolved around the circle in the opposite direction. And finally, two other members circled the campfire four times, as a hunter and a deer, representing the hunt for food during the year.

On the forth revolution, the hunter symbolically shoots the deer and then gives thanks to the Gods for the food, shelter, and health of his people.

This was a simple, but very important dance that was their way of praying and saying thanks for what they had. How do you "say thanks" for what you have? What do you do that shows your appreciation for the food, shelter, and health that you and your family enjoy? Most of us say "Grace" at meals, our way of saying thanks for our food, and perhaps a little prayer at church for the health and happiness we have. Maybe you can come up with a special way you can say thanks for what we are enjoying here today. Perhaps a simple dance or song that says "Thank you Lord."

Month 12
Christmas
A Wonderful Time of Year

Have you ever noticed that things are different in December? People are happier, lots of things are happening, and everyone rushes around trying to get things done. I think it's always been special because it's Christmas time.

We all have great expectations for the holidays, friends and families getting together, buying gifts, singing songs, and enjoying the festivities that go along with the season. It truly is a wonderful time of year.

The true spirit of Christmas is within us, buried deep within our souls, embedded in our hearts from birth. We are grateful for the good tidings that the year has brought us, and give thanks for the blessings we have received.

Even if circumstances aren't exactly the way we would like them to be, we make the best of the Christmas season with our love and understanding of the people around us, and help spread the joys of Christmas with our hearts and the feeling we have for others.

Yes, the true "Spirit of Christmas" isn't how much you spend on someone, or how great a gift you give or receive, but is how much love, joy, and happiness you can spread during this time of the year. Our love toward our friends and family is the greatest gift we can give, the joy we spread honors our God, and the happiness we receive is our reward.

May God Bless You.

Happy Birthday Jesus.

CHAPTER
3

12 Monthly Leader Minutes

Month 1
The Scoutmaster

There isn't any pay for you, you serve without reward.
The boys who tramp the fields with you but little could afford.
And yet your pay is richer far than those who toil for gold,
For in a dozen different ways your service shall be told.

You'll read it in the faces of a Troop of growing boys.
You'll read it in the pleasure of a dozen manly joys.
And down the distant future – you will surely read it then,
Emblazoned thru the service of a band of loyal men.

Five years of willing labor and of brothering a Troop,
Five years of trudging highways, with the Indian cry and whoop,
Five years of camp fires burning, not alone for pleasure's sake,
But the future generation which the boys are soon to make.

They have no gold to give you, but when age comes on to you,
They'll give you back the splendid things you taught them how to do.
They'll give you rich contentment and a thrill of honest pride,
And you'll see your nation prosper, and you'll all be satisfied.

– by Edgar A. Guest

Month 2
The Bridge Builder

An old man, going a lone highway,
came at the evening, cold and gray,
to a chasm, vast and wide and steep,
with waters rolling cold and deep.

The old man crossed in the twilight dim,
that sullen stream had no fears for him,
but he turned when safe on the other side,
and built a bridge to span the tide.

"Old Man," said a fellow pilgrim near,
"You are wasting your strength with building here.
Your journey will end with the ending day;
you never again will pass this way.
You have crossed the chasm, deep and wide,
why build you this bridge at eventide?"

The builder lifted his old gray head.
"Good friend, in the path I have come," he said,
"there followeth after me today,
a youth whose feet must pass this way.

This chasm that was as naught to me,
to that fair haired youth may a pitfall be,
he too must cross in twilight dim,
good friend, I am building this bridge for him."

— by Wm. Allen Dromgoole

Month 3
Like Yesterday

I know when I was small, you'd watch me all the time,
Peeking in to see me sleep, making sure that I was fine,
Then when I started walking, you loved to see me play,
I wish you'd spend some time with me like you did yesterday.

And then when I was five, you taught me how to throw,
I asked a million questions about things I didn't know,
You always took the time to help me everyday,
I wish you'd spend some time with me like you did yesterday.

But now that I am ten, you can't seem to find the time,
To help me with my homework, or watch me when I climb,
Your TV programs too important, football's great you say,
I wish you'd spend some time with me like you did yesterday,

And when I joined the Scouts, and played baseball at my school,
I wished you'd get involved, but instead you played it cool,
Hey Mom and Dad, did you know I scored, and did you see me play?
I wish you'd spend some time with me like you did yesterday,

And when I became a teen, I really needed to know,
Another million questions, but now where did you go?
Your job, TV, and other things, you never seem to stay,
I wish you'd spend some time with me like you did yesterday,

At 16 I tried to fight the world, I thought that I was cool,
But every time I talked to you, you treated me like a fool,
It's no wonder I rejected you and didn't want to stay,
I wish you'd spent some time with me like you did yesterday.

The problems I now face today could have easily been resolved,
If only you had taken the time and really got involved,
But that time has passed and it's too late, it's hard to hear you say,
"We wish we spent some time with you like we did yesterday."

– by Dave Tracewell

Month 4
Within My Power

I am not a very important person, as Importance is commonly rated. I do not have great wealth, control a big business, or occupy a position of great honor or authority.

Yet, I may someday mold destiny. For it is within my power to become the most important person in the world in the life of a boy. And every boy is a potential atom bomb in human history.

All about me are boys. They are the makers of history, the builders of tomorrow. If I can have some part in guiding them up the trail of Scouting, on to the high road of noble character and constructive citizenship, I may prove to be the most important person in their lives, the most important person in my community.

A hundred years from now it will not matter what my bank account was, the sort of house I lived in, or the kind of car I drove. But the world may be different, because I was important in the life of a boy.

– by Forest Witcraft

Month 5
A Scoutmaster's Dream

The Scoutmaster sat in a big chair and groaned.
His weekend camping ended, at last he was home.
Tonight he could sleep in his own nice soft bed,
No shouts from the Scouts would ring in his head.
A hot bath and then he was soon fast asleep,
Content, for tonight—no vigil to keep.

But somehow in dreamland great men he did meet.
They called him by name as he walked down the street.
At first he was puzzled; now who could they be?
And then he remembered—Scout Camporees!
The lads were grown men now, no longer just boys,
The lines on their faces showed sorrows and joys.

His heart was made glad, they remembered his name;
Perhaps all his scouting has not been in vain.
The nights by the campfire, the stars in the sky,
The hands held in reverence "On my Honor"pledge I.
The boys of today, men tomorrow will be,
And the Scoutmaster's dream fulfilled, we shall see.

– by Mrs. Mildred Goodwin

Month 6
The Impact Of Scouting

Since 1907, when Baden-Powell first started the Scouting movement, there has been over 300 million youth world wide that have been a part of the Scouting Movement. During that period one must ask the question: what effect has Scouting had on these youth?

What impact has the ideals and methods of the Boy Scout program had on these youth? Here are some interesting statistics that provide some of these answers:

Boy Scout Alumni are:
   71% of football captains
   65% of basketball captains
   85% of student council presidents
   88% of school newspaper editors
   77% of editors of school annuals
   75% of business managers of school publications
   80% of junior class presidents
   89% of senior class presidents
   65% of college graduates
   72% of Rhodes scholars
   75% of Military Academy graduates
   65% of U.S. Congress
   85% of Airline Pilots
   85% of F.B.I. Agents
   26 of the first 29 astronauts.
   11 of the 12 who walked on the moon.
   108 of 172 astronauts were Boy Scouts.
   Over half of the 108 attained Star, Life, or Eagle rank.

For every 100 Youths involved in Scouting
12 will have their first contact with a church.
5 will earn their religious emblem.
1 will enter the clergy
1 will use Scout skills to save a life.
1 will use Scout skills to save his own life.
2 will become Eagle Scouts.
8 will enter professions first learned through the Merit Badge system.
17 will become Scouting volunteers and pass their skills, inspiration, and leadership to countless youth.
18 will develop hobbies that will give them lifelong interest.
Only rarely will one ever appear in juvenile court.
And yet, SCOUTING reaches only 25% of the youth in the United States.

These figures taken from the Jan/Feb. 1991 issue of Scouter's Digest

Month 7
The Magic Pipes

"*A tiny flame on Brownsea, just the spark of an idea,*
In the mind of one who could both dream and act.
Just the lilt of distant piping, drawing boys from far and near,
And the Brotherhood of Scouting was a fact.
And we followed with the others for we could not stay away
And the piper led us onward on a new untrodden way.
And the magic of his piping and its echo haunt us yet,
Through good and ill, across the crowded years.
We can hear it in the silences, and never quite forget
Those early camps, those youthful hopes and fears.
We can hear the distant echo as we climb the steepest hill,
And an echo can be precious now the magic pipes are still.
They led to high adventure with that little Troop of boys
Who followed us along the Scouting trail.
They led to stilly moonlight and the Camp Fire's fun and noise
And sunset by the river in the dale.
They led to mirth and laughter, to humility and prayer,
They led us up the chancel to the Presence that is there.
They led to precious friendships which have lasted all our days,
Though half a world may stretch its length between.
They led to kindly tolerance – respect for other ways
Than those which we have trod and proved and seen.
They led above the swamp of life to wider views above,
They showed us better ways to live, and finer things to love.
The lilting music died away and left us on our own,
To tramp our chosen way amid the hills,
To teach our younger brothers the good Scouting we have known,
To lead that they in turn may know its thrills.
So may we pay the debt we owe before the echoes fade,
And thank God for the piper, and the magic that he played..... "

– by Hugh Bloare

Reprinted from "The Scouter" magazine, July 1957

Month 8
Our Future Leaders

What are we doing here? Have you thought about what we are trying to accomplish? In order for us, as adult leaders, to be effective, we must define our roles, know our place, and follow our plans to develop the youth in our Unit. This is the Boy Scouts of America, and we are here to help our youth learn to be the leaders of tomorrow. We do that by first training them to be leaders, trusting them to do the job, and then, the most important part, and often the hardest, is to let them be leaders.

Our roles as Adult Leaders, Committee Members, Merit Badge Counselors, and a multitude of other adult positions are simply that of first, trainers, and then support personnel. We are here to help the Scouts be leaders, NOT to lead them.

Our "place" in the Unit organization is that of advisors, trainers, and supporters of what the Youth come up with as a program. We can make suggestions, define realistic parameters and goals, and let them know what resources are available, but then we need to let them, the Youth in our unit, decide what they want and can do for their programs, events, and outings.

After they make a plan that is realistic and attainable, it is up to us, as adults, to make sure that we come up with the help and support to make it happen. We need to encourage our youth to follow though with the plans they make, seek training opportunities, and most important, have fun with the program. Baden-Powell said: "If it ain't fun, it ain't Scouting!" They need to know that it is their program, and that they, the youth of our unit, are in charge of the program, not the adults!

Baden-Powell also said something else about Youth Leaders that is as appropriate now as it was 80 years ago...

"Train Them, Trust Them, and then Let Them lead."

Month 9
What is this Success?

What is this success, that a man should be?
Is it money all around and things that we can see?
Is it cars, and houses, jewels and rings,
that shows a man is a success at things?

To the man whose life revolves 'round these things,
No real happiness does it always bring,
for the wealthiest men of us all may be,
Are those men whose gifts to life were free.

And the man who loves to live that way,
may now be loved in many ways.
A love of all nature ways he shares,
has brought him the love of those who care.

It's he who declares that his wealth now lies,
Not in his wallet, but in his friends and allies,
For it is they who now recall his name,
His wallet not accountable for his fame.

Now when his time has come to leave,
No regrets in this world, do not bereave,
for if he dies with riches a plenty,
It was a waste of life for all his money.

His wealth will not be remembered as well
as what he did, that's what they'll tell.
His friends, family, and the people who care,
Will remember his life, and his love that he shared.

For its he who good people now respect,
and it's he they love and not reject,
And it's he who gives more than he receives,
That is his success, his true belief,

— by Dave Tracewell

Month 10
The Permanence of Scouting

I have seen many times how some parents, in their love and zeal to see their young Scout succeed, "take over" on a project or event, so that their Scout will "look good" or not fail. No one likes to watch their children struggle or fail, it's common nature to want to jump right in and help... I was guilty of the same thing myself until a wise old Scoutmaster, and friend, came up to me one day and told me it was "Okay" to let them fail.

I watched as he walked over to one Scout who was pitching a tent and stood there silently as the Scout repeatedly tried to tie a taut-line hitch. After a few failed tries the Scout asked him if he would tie it for him, the Scoutmaster just smiled gently and said "No." The Scout, now a bit frustrated tried again, but failed. He then asked the Scoutmaster if he would show him how to tie the knot... the Scoutmaster smiled again and said "of Course," showed the Scout how to tie the knot, watched him tie it correctly a couple of times, and then walked away. The Scout never forgot how to tie a taut-line hitch again.

Too many parents are in such a rush to "make" their children successes, that they jump in and do the work themselves without letting their child learn by failing. It is "okay" to let them fail as long as they have the means to succeed. This will help to teach them persistence and tenacity in achieving their goals. As parents, we are prone to want to protect our children from all of lives little problems.

We want to "make things better" and make the "bad things" go away. The methods used in the Scouting program gives us an opportunity to protect our children by teaching them and letting them learn how to succeed though a series of tests and advancements that "allows" them to fail until they do succeed.

The ideals and values taught in the Scouting program offers our children an "Umbrella of Protection" in dealing with many of lifes little problems. They are exposed to many areas of interest and things that they would not normally come in contact, and are taught how to safely approach them. They are taught how to safely handle a knife and ax, how to build and start fires, that you need to have a buddy while swimming, wear a life jacket when they are in a boat, wear their seat belts in your car, and a thousand other things designed into the program to help the Scouts deal with lifes problems with they occur.

The protection is built into the program for the Scouts to learn and have the rest of their lives. Remember, Mom and Dad won't always be there to "make things better..." but what they have learned in the Scouting program will be with them for life.

Month 11
Scouting:
A Program Worth Keeping

The Boy Scout organization has, for the last 89 years, provided millions of young men in this country with the most outstanding youth program available in the world. Its programs have always stressed the building of moral strength and character in our young men, instilling a strong sense of citizenship and devotion to their country, and developing their physical strengths. The methods used by the Boy Scouts of America incorporate local civic minded organizations and public institutional programs like School PTA's and local churches to see that these aims are achieved. The basic beliefs of the Boy Scout organization, which include Duty to God, and Duty to Country, have endured many attacks over the years,

These beliefs are critical to the success of our country and it is up to us, as responsible adults, to make sure the program survives and flourishes.

The ideals of the Boy Scouts of America are much too important! Our youth, boys and girls alike, need this type of solid commitment from the volunteers in their community to help keep them from the ravages of the streets.

The BSA's stance on anti-drug programs, child abuse, non-denominational religious beliefs, and anti-gay policies are solid, good rules that we should all heartily accept, endorse, and support in our community and nation.

In 1915, when Scouting was just 7 years old, the President of the United States then, President Woodrow Wilson, said this about Scouting:

"It is fine to have the boys of the country organized for the purposes the Boy Scouts represent, and whenever I see a group of them I am proud of their manliness, and feel cheered by the knowledge of what their organization represents."

The Boy Scout organization represents good, basic, moral values in this community, this country, and around the world, and focuses on many of the problems that face our youth today. It has helped millions of youth world wide to become better aware of their environment, better educated, and "morally straight" in their beliefs.

It is up to us, volunteers like myself, and the thousands of people in this country like yourself, to make these values, sustained by the Scout Law, which proclaims a Scout is "Trustworthy, loyal, helpful, friendly, courteous, kind, obedient, cheerful, brave, clean, and reverent," real and important to the youth in our unit.

Month 12
Baden-Powell's Last Message to Scout Leaders

To my BROTHER SCOUTERS AND GUIDES:

Cecil Rhodes said at the end of his life (and I, in my turn, feel the truth of it), "So much to do and so little time to do it." No one can hope to see the consummation, as well as the start, of a big venture within the short span of one lifetime.

I have had an extraordinary experience in seeing the development of Scouting from its beginning up to its present stage. But there is a vast job before it. The Movement is only now getting into its stride. (When I speak of Scouting I include in it Guiding also.) The one part which I can claim as mine towards promoting the Movement is that I have been lucky enough to find you men and women to form a group of the right stamp who can be relied upon to carry it on to its goal.

You will do well to keep your eyes open, in your turn, for worthy successors to who you can, with confidence, hand on the torch. Don't let it become a salaried organization: keep it a voluntary movement of patriotic service. The Movement has already, in the comparatively short period of its existence, established itself onto a wide and so strong a footing as to show most encouraging promise of what may be possible to it in the coming years.

Its aim is to produce healthy, happy, helpful citizens, of both sexes, to eradicate the prevailing narrow self interest; personal, political, sectarian and national, and to substitute for it a broader spirit of self sacrifice and service in the cause of humanity; and thus to develop mutual good will and cooperation not only within our own country but abroad, between all countries. Experience shows that this consummation is no idle or fantastic dream, but is a practicable possibility if we work for it; and it means, when attained, peace, prosperity and happiness for all. The "encouraging promise" lies in the fact that the hundreds of thousands of boys and girls who are learning our ideals today will be the fathers and mothers of millions in the near future, in whom they will in turn inculcate the same ideals provided that these are really and unmistakably impressed upon them by the leaders of today.

Therefore you, who are Scouters and Guiders, are not only doing a great work for your neighbor's children, but are also helping in practical fashion to bring to pass God's Kingdom of peace and goodwill upon earth. So, from my heart, I wish you Godspeed in your effort.

– Baden-Powell of Gillwell

ACKNOWLEDGEMENTS

I would like to thank and acknowledge The Scouts of Troop 60 in Lodi, CA for providing me my stage to deliver these and many other Scoutmaster's minutes. It is my true wish that they have somehow become better men from these moments.

I would also like to acknowledge William "Green Bar Bill" Hillcourt for his tremendous contributions to Scouting, and his inspirations, through the official Boy Scout Handbook that helped me focus on the Scouts and their needs.

And to The Boy Scouts of America, for graciously allowing me to use some of their Scouting clip art in this book and for providing the best youth program in the world… a million thanks from me and the millions of Scouts and Scouters they've served.

Bibliography:

The Official Boy Scout Handbook – all editions

The Scoutmaster's Handbook – BSA publication 6501

The many members of the FidoNet Scouter & Scouting Echoes who have given me more Scouting information than I could ever remember, my heartfelt thanks.

Paul Ferris; The Scouter's Digest Newsletter

And the writings of::
    Wm. Allen Dromgoole
    Edgar A. Guest
    Forest Witcraft
    Mrs. Mildred Goodwin
    Hugh Bloare

The Bible:
NASV = New Testament Standard Version
KJV = King James Version
RSV = Revised Standard Douay Version

The Scouter Magazine – The Magic Pipes
Lord Robert Baden-Powell – Drawings and sketches